Annie Armstrong's Amazing Adventures

ROSALIE HALL HUNT

Annie Armstrong's Amazing Adventures

© 2025 Rosalie Hall Hunt

All Rights Reserved

ISBN 978-1-955295-64-2

Cover:
    Background — A Kiowa village scene in Oklahoma Territory
    Artist's rendition of the young Annie Armstrong — Work by Avis Chisam, Huntsville, AL

Cover design:
    Eric J. Hudiburg. Justusproductions.org

100 Manly Street
Greenville, South Carolina 29601

PRINTED IN THE UNITED STATES OF AMERICA

Endorsements

With grace and grit, Annie Armstrong paved paths where none had dared to walk. Author Rosalie Hunt paints a vivid picture of a legacy movement that echoes through the ages. Rosalie crafts scenes so rich and clear you feel as though you are sitting in the middle of the dialogue. Pick up this book and step into the story. Relive the moments that made history.

Sandy Wisdom-Martin
Executive Director-Treasurer
Woman's Missionary Union, SBC

Annie Armstrong is one of the most pivotal personalities in the history of Woman's Missionary Union. Her bravery, boldness, passion and persistence are legendary. Annie's life was remarkable, and Rosalie does an amazing job of bringing her to life for generations to come.

Connie Dixon
President
Woman's Missionary Union, SBC

In a time when most women had no voice, Annie stepped forward as a bold leader helping to shape Southern Baptists into a missional force reaching the United States and the world for Christ. How exciting to see this remarkable woman brought to life again for a new generation!

Peg Jones
Chief Development Office
North American Mission Board

Annie Armstrong is a name many Southern Baptists easily recognize, and because of this new look at her life, her legacy is now even more accessible to kids and families. Rosalie Hunt is a master storyteller telling the story of a woman of faith, leadership and a love for our SBC missionaries. I am excited children of all ages will be inspired by learning more about Annie's life and legacy!

Heather Keller
Missions Consultant
Girls in Action/Children in Action/Acteens
National Woman's Missionary Union

Annie Armstrong's life and commitment to the gospel is inspiring. She was the first executive director of Woman's Missionary Union. But her greatest and most endearing contribution was her undying energy and passion for evangelism. In her own words, "What a glorious thing to be a coworker with God in winning the world for Christ." Rosalie Hunt records her amazing life. It's a story every child needs to hear!

Tim Dowdy
Vice President for Evangelism
North American Mission Board

Annie Armstrong is my hero. She worked to help Native American women organize for missions. She rallied women to support missionaries in Native American territory. In 1900, Annie made a 4,000-mile, forty-day trip to Oklahoma in hopes of unifying work in the territory. She returned repeatedly, making five trips to the territory, traveling by train, carriage and on horseback. As a child, I played on the rock Annie used in mounting her horse during her visit!

Augusta (Gus) Smith
North American Link
Director of Native Praise Choir

Dedication

In loving memory of Annie Armstrong,
WMU's remarkable pioneer leader,
and to the amazing women
who have followed in her train

Table of Contents

Foreword i
Preface iii
Acknowledgments vii
Chapter One .... A Country At War: 1861 1
Chapter Two .... Growing Up: 1868 11
Chapter Three .... A Fresh Beginning: 1873–1881 21
Chapter Four .... Something New: 1882–1887 33
Chapter Five .... Go Forward! 1887–1888 43
Chapter Six .... WMU Is Born: 1888–1890 53
Chapter Seven .... Annie and the New Arrivals: 1890s 65
Chapter Eight .... Go West, Miss Annie! 1896–1901 75
Chapter Nine .... Travels Near and Far: 1901–1902 87
Chapter Ten .... Topsy Turvy Times: 1903–1906 99
Epilogue 111
Bibliography 117

Foreword

You likely know a bit about Annie Armstrong — or at least contribute to the offering named in her honor — if you selected this book to add to your collection.

As a Baptist journalist and longtime missions advocate, I'm familiar with the basics of Armstrong's life and ministry, and I've used countless references to her through the years in various published articles.

What I didn't know was the depth of the layers of her life that helped develop the person she would become, which, in turn, played a major part in shaping Southern Baptist life. What I did know, however, was that if anyone could transport us back into the 1800s and early 1900s to help us capture the full picture of who she was, it would be Rosalie Hunt.

Hunt is fascinated with missions history and dives in deep to fully understand and report back to us what she learns. Her storytelling ability is a natural gift and she's been sharing the missions story, especially as it relates to Baptists, her entire adult life. And while she delivers her captivating tales orally as well as through the written word, it's only been in her later years that she's put these stories to paper in the form of books.

With this publication, she is the author of eleven books along with thousands of articles, reports, monologues and other messages.

The daughter of missionaries to China, Hunt and her husband, Bob, served for thirty years as missionaries to eight Asian nations, including China, Hong Kong, Taiwan and Burma (Myanmar). She is sought after nationally and internationally for events representing the Judson family's connection to Burma.

She also received honorary doctorates from Judson University in Elgin, Illinois, and Judson College, which was in Marion, Alabama, because of her deep admiration, respect and knowledge of Adoniram and Ann Judson.

Hunt also has a special "devoted patron award" named in her honor by WMU Foundation because of her consistent gifts to missions funds and for allowing the proceeds of many of her books to go toward supporting missions endeavors.

Hunt is a past president of Alabama WMU, served five years as national WMU recording secretary, and is a former board member of WMU Foundation and TAB Media Group, which publishes The Alabama Baptist and The Baptist Paper.

You'll find a reference to when Armstrong wrapped up her time as leader of national Woman's Missionary Union in 1906 in Hunt's account in this book.

She describes Armstrong as "possibly the most recognizable of any name in North American missions," and she references a state Baptist paper editor's account of Armstrong.

"The name 'Annie Armstrong' will always be a household word among Southern Baptists, and her memory will be frequent through the long years to come," the editor wrote. "Through her life and the forces she put in motion, this pioneer woman's missions leader left a great legacy to Southern Baptists."

Hunt noted how the editor would have had no idea that his was a prophetic voice.

Another who doesn't realize, and likely can't comprehend, the magnitude of her influence, nurturing and inspiration for the missions story is Rosalie Hunt.

Jennifer Davis Rash
President and Editor-in-Chief
The Alabama Baptist and The Baptist Paper

Preface

I have heard the name Annie Armstrong ever since I was a five-year-old Sunbeam (Mission Friend) living in Temple, Texas, during World War II. I thought I knew a bit about her after researching and writing the history of Woman's Missionary Union in 2013. (*We've A Story to Tell: 125 Years of WMU,* commemorated WMU's 125th anniversary.) In recent years, I've learned a wealth more. Yet, in some ways, Annie is more a puzzle to me than she was in the beginning. I stand in awe of her dedication and remarkable commitment to God's call on her life. She left a permanent imprint on Baptist history. Studying her life and response to God's call on her has made me more sensitive to how each of us must listen to that still, small voice He has implanted in our hearts.

Then and now, Annie Armstrong was not easily ignored. People she worked with did not always agree with her. Even now, some of us might not like all her decisions. We easily find her a puzzle and often do not understand her actions. But, we cannot ignore her. Not one time in the intensive research I have made into her life have I doubted the sincerity of her love for God and commitment to His service. Some Baptist leaders found her austere; others found her all business. Everyone found her brilliant and creative. Children adored her. They did not view her as a tall, regal, larger-than-life leader. She was their Miss Annie, who loved them and stood for no nonsense and would do anything in the world for them. Furthermore, she gave them wonderful tea parties and taught them how to talk to God.

In researching this fascinating woman, I wanted to learn about her childhood and how it felt to grow up in a well-to-do home in the years prior to the War Between the States. Finding information about her immediate family proved very difficult. Little was written. It isn't even certain what private schools Annie attended. Nonetheless, it is extremely clear that she had a broad, thorough education and a brilliant mind that absorbed knowledge like a sponge. Few details are written about her immediate family, including her parents and her siblings. It is apparent that the Armstrong children were privileged. It is also obvious that they learned at their mother's knee the importance of serving others, and, above all, serving God.

Losing her father before she was even two years old must have profoundly affected Annie. If there was an uncle who served as a father figure, we don't know. We can only guess. We can certainly know that her mother, Mary Armstrong, was a remarkably loving and caring mother. She lived before her children what it meant to be devoted to God. That is how she raised her children. She could not have known how famous her youngest daughter would one day be, or how she would influence not just her own generation but the generations to come.

Annie Armstrong's love of children is clear. Spending time with her Sunday school students was her great joy. It is also apparent that she actually loved work. Being idle was a foreign idea to her. Writing was fun. So was office work and organizing papers and creating ideas and putting them to work. The more I read, the more I realized that her sister Alice was a huge part of her great success as the founding leader of Woman's Missionary Union. Where Annie was, Alice wasn't far away. She stood by Annie, encouraged her, supported her, and "propped her up on her leaning side," as the old expression puts it. Alice was the opposite of Annie in many ways. Annie often spoke before she thought. Alice was calm and measured and always thought things through. Alice was the great encourager. She did not want the limelight. She preferred to work in the background. Both sisters were clearly brilliant. What an amazing team they were.

Annie never accepted a salary. Nor did Alice. They felt their work in missions was their gift to God. It may have been difficult for them to understand that everyone else could not work the same way. The Armstrong girls had been raised in an affluent home and had never had to want for anything. However, they never felt entitled. Just the opposite. They felt that their blessings were given to them so that they could, in turn, pass them on. Their personalities were alike in some ways, and completely opposite in others. Teamwork came naturally to them.

Annie broke new ground for Baptists and inspired thousands of fellow Baptists, young and old. Join me in exploring the life and heart of this amazing woman. She changed and shaped an entire denomination. Her life stands to inspire us to see just what God has in His plan for us as well.

Acknowledgments

Can an author ever find a better friend than an archivist who loves her work? That is just the treasure Woman's Missionary Union has in Cindy Goodwin at WMU archives. The writer's quest becomes Cindy's quest, and it becomes special teamwork. WMU is blessed. So am I.

Just as valuable is a leader who loves history, even while she is making it herself. That is just what WMU has in Sandy Wisdom-Martin, our national director. The story is, that if Sandy is not out doing her work across the nation, she is in the WMU building in Birmingham. And, the story goes, that if she isn't in her office, the quickest way to find her is to visit the archives and find her delving into missions history.

Another writer's friend is located in the office of our national children's consultant. Heather Keller is the all-in leader of all things children and missions. She loves her work, and it shows. And she loves helping those who are working with children and material for them. What a team we have at national WMU!

Not only there, but at the International Mission Board in Richmond, Kyndal Owens is an archivist par excellence. You just give her a name, or a setting, or a date, and she can quickly help you find just the right letter or information about some figure in our missions history.

There are several living authors who have extensively studied Annie Armstrong's story, and they have been a tremendous help. Bobbie Sorrill wrote the definitive biography of Annie Armstrong more than forty years ago, and it is a treasure trove of interesting information.

More recently, about two decades ago, Cathy Butler wrote a captivating account of Annie Armstrong. (I have the honor of saying I taught Cathy Butler in my seventh grade World History class, and she was a brilliant student!)

I have been blessed with assistance from several eminent historians. I don't think I have written any book in which I did not receive invaluable information and help from Catherine Allen of Birmingham, Alabama.

One of the valuable leads Dr. Allen passed on to me was to contact Dr. Karen O'Dell Bullock, distinguished professor of Christian Heritage at B.H. Carroll Theological Seminary. She shared with me the fascinating history of Baptist missions work with indigenous tribes in Oklahoma during Annie Armstrong's day.

Ever since 2011, I have been blessed with an editor who is a Baptist, a retired WMU editor, and a skilled reader of manuscripts. She has the gift of taking a confusing sentence and helping it make sense. Ella Robinson is a gifted editor and a treasured friend. Another gifted friend serves as long-time editor at Courier Publishing. Denise Huffman has been rendering talented and gracious assistance for eight books now.

In all the books written in the past ten years, I have been blessed with a talented grandson who is in media and marketing. Eric Hudiburg has a gift with pictures, design, color, and covers. I am blessed to have his talent available.

With it all, there is the blessing of readers of several generations who always want to learn more about the wonderful women and men who have been called by God to take His message to the world. There is always something new and fascinating to learn, and a new generation of readers who wants to hear the old, old story and make it their own.

Annie Armstrong's Amazing Adventures

Sater's Church. Oldest Baptist church in Maryland, built in 1742 by Henry and Dorcas Sater, Annie Armstrong's great-great-grandparents. (Courtesy of Betty Brown, member of the church)

Chapter One

A COUNTRY AT WAR
1861

Annie turned from the window in the front room, anxiously calling out, "Mama, do you know why is there so much noise in the street? Come look! All the people are hurrying toward downtown Baltimore!"

Mary Armstrong came quickly from the large kitchen and stood next to Annie. They both peered intently at the commotion outside. Mary marveled again at how tall her youngest daughter had gotten. Only 10, Annie was already nearly as tall as her mother. Annie's father had been exceptionally tall, and Annie was clearly taking after him.

Mary looked puzzled as she watched the growing crowd of people. "Mama," Annie's voice sounded concerned, "everybody looks worried."

"Yes, most unusual," Mary responded. "James John," Mary called out to her only son, "please come quickly." In moments, James, who had just celebrated his twelfth birthday the week before, came bounding down the stairs.

"Son, please go quickly to your Uncle Eugene's house and ask for news. The activity out here in the street is strange," she explained. James loved to run errands, and going to Uncle Eugene's house always gave him an excuse to see his twin cousins. The young Levering boys were already teenagers, and he looked up to them.

True to his task, James hurried the few blocks to his aunt and uncle's fine home. Ann Levering was his mama's closest sister, and Annie was her namesake. The families were often together. Uncle Eugene was a wealthy Baltimore businessman and shipowner, and James was fascinated with the sea.

In short order, James returned, accompanied by Uncle Eugene himself. Mary Armstrong quickly ushered them in, asking anxiously about all the confusion in their usually quiet neighborhood. Eugene looked troubled as he shared what he knew.

"I'm concerned as well, Mary. I have just received a message from my office that a riot is happening on Pratt Avenue!"

A riot? As she heard the word, Annie's heart skipped a beat. "What is causing a riot, Uncle Eugene?" Annie looked anxiously into his eyes.

"Annie, it seems Union soldiers were marching down Pratt Avenue," he explained, "and people who are Southern sympathizers started throwing rocks and bricks at them." Mary and Annie both gave a little gasp as Eugene Levering explained, "It looks like the first deadly shot of a civil war has actually just occurred right here in Baltimore. Last week, Fort Sumter in Charleston was fired on, but there were no injuries. But today, several have died here in Baltimore. God, help us all." He drew a deep breath and finished, "God, help our nation."

Annie gave a gulp as she thought: *This is real. This isn't just a story. Our own nation may be at war.* Although she was just 10 years old, Annie was a serious and gifted student. She was really good at mathematics, and she loved history as well. Uncle Eugene's news was deeply troubling to her. She felt like she was living in history that she wished was not happening.

Annie Armstrong's life had been mostly quiet and sheltered until this point. Not that life had been easy. Annie had been too young to realize the tragedy that hit her family when she was just 18 months old. James Armstrong, her tall, strong, handsome father, was only 46 years old when he died quite suddenly. Then, when she was 7, sorrow again entered their Baltimore home. Several of the Armstrong children, including Annie and her little 5-year-old brother William, were playing in the park with other neighborhood youngsters. A larger boy roughly pushed William, knocking him down and seriously injuring him. William died a few days later, and the family was heartbroken.

Annie never forgot what occurred less than a week later. Even as tears trickled down her cheeks, Mary Armstrong gathered her three daughters and one remaining son around her. "Children," and her voice caught in her throat, "I am asking you to never mention what happened to your brother. It would ruin that larger boy's life, and we have already had enough sorrow to last a lifetime." Annie was still a young child, but she never forgot her mother's depth of concern for others, even over something so difficult to forgive.

A city girl, Annie loved growing up in Baltimore. In the mid-1800s, Baltimore was the third largest city in the United States. It was a wonderful location for a city, with its excellent harbor and fertile land. In this year, 1861, Baltimore bustled with people, businesses, and possibilities. Carriages, horses, carts, and people filled the streets and sidewalks of the city. Many thousands of immigrants flooded into America through Baltimore's harbor. When Annie walked down the street, she often heard ten or twelve different languages spoken along the way. She was intrigued by the many immigrant children she saw. Annie always wondered what it felt like to be in a strange place like Baltimore. *What would it be like to be surrounded by strange sounds and strange faces?* She felt sorry for them, especially the children. It must be hard to be a stranger and always feel somehow different. (These thoughts were always in Annie's mind. Later in her life, she did a lot of things to help little children who were foreigners in America.)

Annie's father had been a well-to-do merchant. James Armstrong wasn't as wealthy as their relatives, the Leverings, but the family had been quite prosperous. However, there were business setbacks in the year before James Armstrong died. After James died, Annie's mother became the head of the business and the household. With her organizational skills and with her sister, Annie Levering, and brother-in-law nearby to advise her, Mary managed quite well.

Annie found Baltimore harbor and the sea fascinating. Brother James was nutty about sailing and couldn't wait to "go to sea." Mama always cautioned him to not rush it, to grow up and diligently study first. That was hard for a rough-and-tumble young boy to do. Annie often sighed and wondered why life seemed so unfair. Boys could do all sorts of exciting things girls were not allowed to do, like travel where you wanted to or work at a fine job. She simply could not understand why girls couldn't do the same. Annie often mused to herself, *Now if I were a boy, I could grow up to be a good businessman. I love numbers, and I'm good with them. But girls can't get jobs. I just don't understand it.*

Nonetheless, going on adventurous trips around Baltimore with James was one of Annie's favorite pastimes. Her big brother might not admit it openly, but Annie was a good sport, always listening to him and letting him lead the way to interesting places around the town. Both children loved going to Uncle Eugene's office near the harbor. The sight of all those large sailing ships and the tantalizing smell of coffee beans from the harbor warehouses made each trip an exciting experience. Another favorite spot for Annie was Federal Hill. From the hill, there was a wonderful view of the harbor flowing out to the sea and of the bustling city far beneath them. Annie always felt "historical shivers" when they topped the hill. This was the very place where Maryland had ratified the US Constitution in 1788. She loved history, and Federal Hill made it come alive for the brilliant young girl.

Back at home, Annie would sometimes have serious talks about life with her sister Alice. Sister could always be counted on to have an ear that really listened. In moments of true honesty, Annie realized that, for her own part, she was more likely to act first rather than listen and think a thing through. She wanted action, not quiet, thinking times. Sister Alice was already 14 and nearly four years older. Nonetheless, the sisters were very close. Alice was quiet and gentle, enjoying writing in her journal or working on a new piece of embroidery. Annie thought needlework took far too much time. She wanted to be up and doing.

Annie also realized that she had a quick temper. Often, she would speak before she thought something through. Mamie, their older sister, was the family beauty and seemed more mature than the rest of the children. All four of them had chores to perform and would not think of refusing to do them. Mama might be quiet and small, but she was the loving leader in the family, and each child respected and honored her.

Annie frequently watched her mother at work with the family budget ledger. She was excellent with numbers and organization, and Annie greatly admired Mama. In turn, Mary Armstrong noticed traits and characteristics of each one of her brood of children. Mamie was good with organizing and running a household. Alice was talented at handwork and was excellent with words. She loved keeping records and writing interesting stories. James was wild about the sea and couldn't wait to "grow up and sail the seven seas." Mary worked hard to keep him focused on studies and learning skills.

Mary recognized Annie's brilliance with mathematics, planning, and organization. Her youngest daughter excelled at school, absorbing knowledge and ideas like a sponge. She was steeped in reading and appreciated the classics in literature. Annie's weak point, however, was languages. She grew really frustrated when studying a foreign language and trying to pronounce words correctly, especially French. Somewhere in the process, Annie simply became convinced languages were not for her. She just could not feel comfortable speaking anything but English.

Mary Armstrong knew that Annie always wanted to be up and doing. Quiet work was not appealing to this quicksilver daughter. In looks and size, Alice took after her father's side of the family. On the other hand, Annie had Mary's large, lustrous brown eyes and lips shaped just like hers. When it came to height, however, Alice already topped their mother by many inches, and Annie was quickly doing the same.

All three daughters enjoyed attending Seventh Place Baptist Church. It had been part of their lives ever since they could remember. Mama was a charter member there. Mamie and Alice remembered their father well. Annie just knew him by the fine portrait of him, with her mama sitting at his side. James Armstrong had been a Presbyterian but gave generously to his wife's Baptist church. Mary was deeply involved with helping needy people, both in their church and city. The children grew up understanding that helping others was an important part of life. God had blessed them, and they needed to pass those blessings along. Annie's family ties to the Baptist church went all the way back to the earliest settlements in Maryland.

Annie loved their yearly pilgrimage to Sater's Baptist Church. Annie was immensely proud that her great-great-grandfather Sater had built the first Baptist church in all of Maryland. This happened well over a hundred years earlier. Young Henry Sater was not yet 20 when he arrived in America in 1709. And Annie's great-great-grandmother, Dorcas, laid the cornerstone of that first church more than a hundred years before Annie's time. Every June, all the different branches of the family drove their buggies eleven or so miles outside Baltimore to Sater's Church for a big anniversary celebration. Some poetic family members called it "Cherry Meeting," because the cherry trees around the little church were heavy with ripe, red cherries when everyone arrived at the church at celebration time. Each year, Annie looked forward to picking ripe cherries and popping them in her mouth, savoring that sweet, red juice.

At "Cherry Meeting" this June, once again, Henry Sater's descendants *descended* on historic Sater's Church. Henry and his lovely young wife, Dorcas, gave the land to the Baptist congregation in the area. He even had the bricks to build it sent from England. That first June, in 1742, family and friends attended the service for the laying of the cornerstone of the church. Lovely young Dorcas Sater herself laid the cornerstone. In those days, women were never recognized in public; however, on this very special occasion, Henry Sater would have it no other way. After all, it had been Dorcas who insisted on having a special place of worship to honor God. Thus, the first Baptist church in all Maryland was dedicated that memorable June Sunday in 1742, with fifty-seven charter members.

The custom each year was for one of the Sater descendants to tell the famous family story. Uncle Eugene was the historian this year, and Annie drank it all in. Here this intrepid ancestor of hers — a woman! — had done something so important. The idea began to take root in Annie's keen young mind: *God could use women, too.* She wanted to do something special with *her* life. The sermon was long, however, and Annie squirmed a bit after sitting and listening so long. She glanced across the aisle to where James was sitting with his cousins. They, too, were noticeably squirming. Annie was already thinking about the marvelous spread of food that all the good cooks had brought. The banquet of food would be set up on tables out under the trees, and everyone would eat their fill.

Nonetheless, Cherry Meeting was a bit subdued this year of 1861. The War Between the States was in full swing, and everyone was uneasy. Brother fought against brother. Maryland was a border state, so sentiment was very mixed. People in north and west Baltimore were more inclined to have Union sympathies. Those in the south and east part of the city were much more likely to lean toward the Confederacy. Just last month, on May 13, Union General Benjamin Butler had quietly led 1,000 Union troops to occupy Federal Hill. Baltimore was placed under martial law, and life changed for everyone. Annie and James no longer had their former freedom to explore Federal Hill or any other spot in a city controlled by martial law. (Martial law meant Union soldiers controlled the city and the times and places where citizens could be.)

Churches were very careful to stay neutral. To show partiality to the Confederacy could bring a charge of treason on a pastor. A pastor could even be arrested. Dr. Richard Fuller was the Armstrongs' pastor at Seventh Place Baptist Church. Fuller grew up in South Carolina and graduated from the famous Harvard University. He was a brilliant preacher and a genuinely loving pastor. Dr. Fuller had to tread a careful line during the war years. Never from the pulpit nor during the week would he discuss North and South and his feelings about the war. When anyone asked if he was "North or South," he invariably responded, "I am a Christian."

Dr. Fuller was beloved of the entire congregation. He was a spellbinding preacher, and Annie never tired of listening each Sunday. Mary said to her family, "Children, what would our Baptist Foreign Mission Board have done without our own Dr. Fuller?"

Annie spoke up, "Mama, tell us the story!"

Mary explained: "With the war going on and on, the sea blockades stopped our missionaries overseas from getting their salaries."

Of course, James' ears perked up at the mention of the sea. "Mama, how can Dr. Fuller help with that?" He sounded puzzled.

Mary replied, "Well, son, Dr. Fuller is president of the Southern Baptist Convention, you know, and a very influential man. He has convinced the United States Secretary of State to allow the funds to come under a flag of truce from headquarters in Richmond to Dr. Fuller here in Baltimore." She drew a satisfied breath and finished, "And he has set up a temporary Foreign Mission Board here in Baltimore. That means he is able to deal with friendly ships' crews here in our harbor who are able to avoid the blockades and get the salaries to our missionaries!" The children were excited to know that their own pastor was helping the missionaries and the foreign board right in the middle of war.

The war dragged on, as did the death and destruction it brought with it. Baltimore worked hard to remain neutral. Annie's family moved when she was 13 years old to 1423 McCulloh Street, a three-story row house closer to where Mary's sister and brother-in-law, Annie and Eugene Levering, lived. Eugene was wonderful with finances and a great help to Mary as she managed what remained of the family fortune.

To Annie, the war seemed to go on forever. In the spring of 1861, many leaders predicted the fighting would be over in weeks. Those weeks turned into months, and the months into *years*. Annie was close to 15 years old when the war, at long last, ended. When peace was finally declared, everyone breathed a sigh of relief. Annie, however, did not feel a true sense of peace. She was full of turmoil inside. It was like her stomach could never really settle down. Life just seemed so uncertain. Annie began to wonder, *Will I ever feel at peace again?*

The Rest of the Story

Baltimore was a wonderful city in which to grow up in the mid-1800s. People from all over the world came to America through Baltimore's harbors. It felt like being a real part of the world. There were all sorts of cultural opportunities and business possibilities, and always something new and exciting to see and experience. Annie's interest in business and leadership grew from going with her mother to market and watching Mary neatly handle the family finances. All the family business decisions were her responsibility. Annie's interests also grew as she watched how the Levering men conducted their business interests. Living in the same neighborhood, the Armstrongs and the Leverings spent a lot of time together. Annie also noted that her mother and the Levering men were not only good business managers but also closely involved in ministry in their church.

As a grown woman, Annie became deeply involved in leading Baptist women all over the United States. All that time, Annie never forgot her early sympathies for the little immigrant children who came to America. They had to learn how to be part of a brand new culture. As a young girl, she had vowed to do something for those children who wanted nothing so much as to belong. Annie never forgot the lessons she learned as a child. She *did* end up making a difference in the lives of many strangers in a new land.

Drawing of Annie Armstrong as a teenager. (Artwork by Avis Chisam, Huntsville, Alabama)

1423 McCulloh Street, Baltimore, where the Armstrongs lived for many years. (Courtesy of National Woman's Missionary Union)

Chapter Two

GROWING UP
1868

As Annie walked to the front door, she paused by the large mirror on the wall. She grinned as her brown eyes focused on the reflection of her straight back and rather regal posture. Mama had asked her two "taller girls" to practice using broomsticks to be their guide in standing straight and proud. Mary Armstrong often laughed as she pointed out her own short height, "Girls, I always wished I could be taller and look elegant. You two are so fortunate to be tall and graceful." She spoke persuasively, "Now use these brooms to be your yardstick for posture and be thankful for God's gift of height!" Both sisters had listened to their mother. Annie actually topped Alice by close to an inch now. They always walked gracefully, drawing admiration from all who saw them. When Mama walked into church with her two younger girls, everyone in the congregation smiled at the sight of petite Mrs. Armstrong heading for "her" pew on the fifth row, followed by her two regal daughters.

In 1865 the war finally came to an end, and Baltimore returned to a much more normal lifestyle. With four teenagers in the house, the Armstrongs frequently invited young people from the church and neighborhood to parties. They had lots of cousins nearby as well. Mother threw open the French doors between the dining room and parlor to make plenty of space. Nora, who cooked for them, made all kinds of goodies to please healthy young appetites. Annie had a good time with all sorts of cousins and friends. Outwardly, she seemed to not have a care in the world. Annie had her share of beaus, but a few of the young men her age were a bit intimidated around the two younger Armstrong sisters who were unusually tall. With most, however, no one thought a thing about it because they were all such good friends. Sister Mamie was going around with stars in her eyes these days. Annie had a feeling that Mamie was in love with their cousin Eugene. She saw the way Eugene looked at Mamie when he visited in their home. Always at family parties, Eugene spent most of his time with Mamie. Of course, they had grown up together, but things had changed now, and both Annie and Alice sensed romance in the air.

Personally, in her heart of hearts, Annie was restless. The country was embracing peace at last, but there was no real peace in her own heart, and she fretted over that. Right before the war ended, Mamie and Alice had professed their faith in Christ and been baptized by Dr. Fuller. Sometimes, Annie noticed Mama looking at her with a question in her eyes. Mary was concerned about her youngest daughter. Annie was unsettled. When she did something she really wanted to do, it was always with all her heart. She knew if she trusted Christ with her life, it would have to be with her whole being. Annie just didn't feel ready to make that sort of commitment. She often thought to herself: *If I commit my life to Christ, then I won't be in control of my life anymore. I know that would be hard to handle.* That was not a comfortable feeling. Annie always liked to be in charge.

However, talking with Mama about life in general and about what she would like to do with her life was easy. Annie admired her mother's quiet competence and assurance. She was amazed at how strong her mother was. It was a physical strength, but, even more, Mama had a strong heart and so much courage. She was raising five children all on her own.

Often in the mornings, Annie would watch Mary sitting at her desk, working on the family's financial records. She carefully entered expenses, credits and debits, managing the family finances with care and skill. "Mama," Annie would sometimes ask, "do you enjoy doing accounts and records?"

Mary frequently replied, "Oh yes, Annie, I am comfortable with figures. They always end up accurately if you manage them in the right way. I feel happy," she smiled and drew a satisfied breath, "when they add up correctly, and I know I have done my job well."

Annie grinned, "Mama, I know that feeling. I love working with numbers, too. They don't try to trick you if you handle them properly. I like things to work the right way — and numbers do that!"

Mary gently smiled, "Annie, I am always so happy when I see how gifted you are with numbers and facts. You handle them with skill and ease."

"Oh, yes, Mama," Annie responded, "I feel like I know what the results will be when I work with numbers." Giving a little shrug, she added, "Now with people, it isn't so easy. I never know how *they* are going to respond! And Mama," Annie continued, "something bothers me. I am so good with business and numbers and planning. But," and the pause was long before she continued, "I'm a girl — a female. I can't go into business like our cousins can. It just doesn't seem fair!"

Mary Armstrong knew that Annie greatly admired her older twin cousins, Josh and Eugene Levering. They were some five years older than Annie, and both had joined their father's thriving shipping business when they were just 16. Here Annie was, over 17, bursting with ability and ambition, but with no visible solution to her problem. She had no outlet for her abilities. Annie sighed, "Mama, I so wish I could work like that. I would be *good* at it, but women just aren't allowed to work in business."

Mary reached over and tenderly touched Annie's arm. "My child," she began, "I have watched you growing up all these years, and I love the talent and energy God has blessed you with. I feel," and she paused significantly, "God has something special in mind for you. He would not have given you these gifts if He did not intend for you to use them," and she patted Annie's arm. "You just watch and keep your eyes open. God will show you His plan."

Annie drew a deep breath as she bent down from her imposing height to softly kiss her mother's cheek. "Mama, I hope you are right. I see how you do God's work all through every week. You set such an example for us."

Annie had been right about her oldest sister, Mamie. Romance was in the air, and 1868 was a big year in the Armstrong home, with a lot of excitement and much change, some good, but some more difficult. Several years earlier, Mary Armstrong had purchased another house on McCulloh Street, one that was closer to her sister, Annie Levering. Annie and her husband, Eugene, were a wonderful help to Mary as she bore the full parental responsibility for raising four children. Annie's sister, Mamie, was the very same age as the Levering twins, and Eugene and Joshua were forever at the Armstrong home. Smiling to herself, Annie thought about the way she and Alice had watched friendship turn to courtship as Mamie

Growing Up: 1868

and Eugene fell in love. The wedding of Mamie and Eugene was the big news of the year in the Armstrong family. The newlyweds set up housekeeping nearby in Baltimore, but Annie and Alice, as well as their brother James, realized that things were different now. The house seemed a bit lonely.

Then came a shock. One morning, the girls came to the breakfast table to find their mother with furrowed brow and clearly working hard to control her emotions. Annie quickly spoke, "Mama, what has happened? Are you all right?"

Mary Armstrong drew a shaky breath. "Girls, James has run away to sea."

"What?" the two girls gasped on the same breath. "James is gone?" Annie burst out.

Mary controlled herself with difficulty, saying, "I always knew he was crazy about going to sea," and she took a deep breath, "but I just wish he had told us first."

For many days, Alice and Annie paid close attention to Mama, giving her an extra helping hand. Slowly, the family adjusted to life without James. When, finally, a letter arrived from James, he said not a word about slipping out without telling them. His letter was full of news of how great it was to sail the seas and have all sorts of new experiences. By unspoken agreement, the two daughters took special pains to assist their mother in ways small and large. They wanted to be there for her. Annie and Alice vowed to never let this dear parent be disappointed in them. It was a vow they kept all the years of Mary Armstrong's long life.

Mrs. Armstrong was a woman who lived her faith. She often talked to her children about thinking for themselves and showing concern for others, but she didn't just talk about it. She lived her own life that way. Her children grew up with a sterling example of loving service in their mother. There was nothing "put on" or pious about Mary; she simply loved and cared for others. She was so respected at their church that she was chosen as president of the Working Society. She supervised the work of the church's many ministries to women. These women went outside the doors of the church and helped their community. The church held regular mothers' meetings for underprivileged women, teaching them how to sew and care for their families. Additionally, Mary led in assisting several organizations in Baltimore that helped the poor, the sick, and the neglected. (It would soon become clear that her organizational skills were inherited by her youngest daughter. Annie became a remarkable leader among women, not just in Baltimore, but all over the United States.)

Now, however, at the ripe old age of 20, Annie was growing more and more restless. It just seemed like she couldn't settle on any one thing she wanted to do. She felt disturbed — so disturbed that she was reluctant to talk about it even to Alice, her dearest friend and confidant. Then one Sunday morning, Annie came to a life-changing decision. It was December 1870, and Annie was seated in her usual pew on the fifth row, waiting for Dr. Fuller to begin his message. His sermon was always the highlight of Sunday worship for Annie. Dr. Fuller had been their pastor for many years, and Annie loved and admired him. When he spoke, she listened. This particular Sunday morning, her restlessness just about overwhelmed her.

Of all things, Dr. Fuller preached today about peace, the very thing that Annie *longed* for but knew she did not have. She listened intently as Dr. Fuller explained, "Everybody has trouble. It may be big. It may be small." It was as if their pastor was speaking directly to her. Annie sat there drinking in each word as he continued, "But what a Christian has is not peace *from* trouble, but peace in the *midst* of trouble." *That is the answer,* Annie immediately thought to herself. *I need Christ right in the middle of my life. I need His peace.*

When the invitation was given, Annie Armstrong resolutely stepped from her pew and walked down the aisle, eager to take Dr. Fuller's hand and tell him that she was committing her life to Christ. Standing just behind her on the fifth pew, her mother shed happy tears for this significant move in her beloved Annie's life. Sister Alice was beaming from ear to ear, and nearby sat their sister Mamie, a smile wreathing her face. They all knew that when Annie committed herself to something, she was in all the way.

As Annie was baptized by Dr. Fuller and became a member of the church, Alice recalled that her sister loved to tell her family and cousins, "Oh, someday I may be a Presbyterian, or possibly a Methodist, but never a Baptist!" The afternoon following Annie's baptism, the two sisters and their mother were sitting around reminiscing about the special events of the previous morning. Alice grinned and reached over to tap Annie's hand, "Sister, I remember you saying you would *never* be a Baptist. Now look at you." Annie laughed as she responded, "Why, Alice, you know I'd never be anything else!"

This was a new Annie Armstrong. She had a purpose now. It was to do whatever God wanted her to do. She looked at every day with fresh, new eyes. That peace she had so longed for was part of her now. So was a new determination to make a difference and do whatever pleased God. Annie didn't know quite what that was, but she prayed each day, asking God to reveal Himself to her. She was willing to serve.

Alice, ever the encourager, said, "Sister, I'm so happy that you have a real purpose now. I've always marveled at your energy. And Annie," she paused and smiled, "I really admire your courage. You are willing to speak your mind and lead out." Annie listened intently; she knew Alice was very observant about people. "Sometimes," Alice continued with the hint of a smile, "you may speak your mind a bit *too* clearly!" Annie grinned in acknowledgment, "I guess that's true, Alice, but I like having you around to sort of keep me in check and give me a look that says, 'Don't speak quite so frankly!' That always helps me. I think we can be a team."

Within just months, the Armstrong women were in a new setting. A large group of the membership of Seventh Place Baptist built and formed a new congregation very near to the Armstrong home. All the Armstrong women became charter members of the new Eutaw Place Baptist Church. The new church building was beautiful, and the women felt part of a fresh, new beginning. It was to be Annie's church home the rest of her long life. At Seventh Place Church, leadership was practically all men, but not so at Eutaw Place. Here, women were on committees, taught classes, and freely used their talents to help others. To make it even better, Dr. Fuller went with the new congregation to be their pastor. All of the Armstrongs felt blessed with this wonderful new church. Life took on real meaning for Annie. Christ was truly her Lord, and she wanted to be whatever God wanted her to be.

This year's Cherry Meeting in June at Sater's Church was the best yet for Annie. Now she was really part of their ancestors' faith, a full partner. It felt good. She belonged. Annie grinned as they walked the familiar path into the centuries-old building constructed by her great-great-grandfather Henry. She moved sedately now but paused at one of the nearby ancient cherry trees. Recalling the spunky little ten-year-old who had climbed this tree to pick some juicy red cherries, the grown up and very tall Annie reached up and gathered in a few without any great effort. Being tall had its good points, she felt. On the inside, Annie still felt spunky and full of anticipation about discovering God's plan for her personally. Annie was on a quest.

The Rest of the Story

Annie never outgrew her fascination with the story of her forebears who founded the first Baptist church in the state of Maryland. Henry Sater was just a teenager when he sailed from England to the area of

Maryland called Chestnut Ridge. Henry farmed tobacco and quickly developed the reputation for being a hard worker — and a strong Baptist. He was nearly 40 when he finally married, and, sadly, his first wife soon died. It was ten years later before he married again, and he and his much younger wife, Dorcas Towson, had six children. By this time, Henry had acquired more than a thousand acres of land.

Just two years after they married, and at Dorcas's urging, Henry built a Baptist meeting house on their property where visiting ministers could preach to those living in the area. He and Dorcas took great pains with the building, even ordering special bricks from England with which to build it. They and some fifty others signed a solemn covenant dedicating the church and surrounding property as being forever a place of worship.

Now, over 200 years later, the church is still there, with a pastor speaking in a warm and welcoming voice, inviting any and all who wish to come worship together. Chestnut Ridge Baptist Church still preserves the original heritage of Sater's Church, with original descendants still in the membership. It has now merged with another congregation from Baltimore, and they have built another structure right next to the original 1742 sanctuary. Very appropriately, the address is 1010 Sater's Lane, at Falls Road. And all these years later, the original cemetery is still in use. Family memories continue to live on. Annie would be happy with that.

Portrait of Alice Armstrong, Annie's sister and dearest friend. (Courtesy of National Woman's Missionary Union)

*Only portrait of Annie Armstrong.
(Courtesy of National Woman's
Missionary Union)*

Chapter Three

A Fresh Beginning
1873–1881

"Sister," Alice spoke with a resigned sigh, "have you *ever* seen a need that you didn't want to do something about?" The Armstrong sisters were walking past Baltimore's Bay View Asylum. As usual, Annie was working on a new idea. She stopped Alice with a touch on her arm. Both sisters paused, looking up at the giant, somewhat foreboding, building on their right.

"But, Alice, can't you just imagine all the hurting people in that asylum who need someone to care about them?" Annie asked.

"Listen, Annie," Alice replied, "you do know that some of those people are out of their minds? I think many of them are addicted to something, and others are just desperately poor and have no other place to live."

"Exactly!" Annie came back. "That is why they need someone to care. I found out just last week that they have no religious service there at all. Alice," and Annie drew a deep breath, "they need to know somebody cares. We could help with a service each week and do something that could make their lives better."

Alice's face crinkled into a smile, "Sister, I figured you already had something spinning around in that creative mind of yours. And yes," she nodded her head in resignation, "I'll help you get this going. I am sure Pastor Fuller will help as well."

Annie happily assured her, "That's what I'm counting on."

That same month, 24-year-old Annie Armstrong organized the Bay View Mission and was soon elected the new organization's president. Once a month, five or six of the young people at Eutaw Place Church would drive a buggy into the country to the city poorhouse, as Bay View was called. Annie often declared, "This must be the greatest opportunity anywhere around here to reach so many unsaved people in one day." (For many years, Annie faithfully carried out this work as she headed up the Bay View Mission.)

Bay View was just one of the many ways the energetic Annie Armstrong was involved in helping others. Her chief assistant was this gentle and quiet sister, unobtrusively at Annie's side, helping in all sorts of practical ways. Annie depended on Alice's quick brain and tactful, kind way of helping people without making a fuss about it. Annie had so many projects that there was never a dull day. Had she not grown up seeing her mama serving others day in and day out? God had blessed their family in all sorts of ways — and the Armstrongs were determined to pass their blessings on.

One of Annie's favorite times each week was her infants Sunday school class. As soon as she had been baptized at Eutaw Place Church, she was asked to teach the infants class. All the children, aged 4 to 14 were called part of the infants class. (For more than fifty years, Annie Armstrong was the leader of the children's ministry at her church.) Children aged 4 to 14 looked up to Miss Annie, both physically and spiritually. Sometimes there were as many as 250 children. Their tall, gracious teacher expected the little ones to obey. They did so out of love and respect, for they could tell Annie loved them. Their Miss Annie knew so much about the Bible, and with her help, they memorized one verse after another. Those children grew up and never forgot the Bible verses, nor the regal, twinkled-eyed teacher who quoted the passages along with the children.

The children's favorite times were the afternoons when Miss Annie and Miss Alice invited them into their home for tea. Those were unforgettable afternoons. Miss Annie always used snowy-white napkins, real tea, and a beautiful teapot. As Miss Alice poured their tea, everyone enjoyed delicious goodies Miss Nora, the Armstrongs' cook, happily prepared for them. And nearly always, before the afternoon was over, Miss Annie was down on the floor, playing jacks with the children.

Annie and Alice also found time every week to have Sunday school on Sunday afternoons at the Home for the Friendless. This was an orphanage for boys and girls who had no parents and were penniless. Every week Annie and Alice, along with some of their church friends, like Jane and Charlotte Norris, would go to the home and teach the 100 children living there. Without fail, after class at the orphanage, Annie would stand at the classroom door and pass out a stick of hard candy to each girl and boy. Each child always got a hug or a pat on the arm along with a special smile. (Many years later, when some of those same children were grown up, they would visit with Miss Armstrong and give her a gift to help pass on treats to the children at the home. The Armstrong sisters planted a lot of seeds in young hearts that grew into flourishing lives in the years to come.)

One Christmas, Annie planned a special program for the children and had a "picture show" of sorts, using a new invention called a stereopticon. It projected pictures on a screen. Many guests had come, and a young man from Annie's church showed the pictures on a wall. All of a sudden, a picture appeared on the wall, and hundreds of young voices called out, "It's Miss Annie!" Unknown to Annie, her church friend decided to pull a prank on Miss Armstrong. He found a picture of her (actually, the only one known to exist) and without Annie's permission, put it in the slide show. Annie was shocked. And Annie was *not* amused. From that time on, never again did she allow her picture to be made or used.

At the same time all these projects were going on, Annie and Alice were becoming part of various missions activities with their mother. Long before the three became charter members of Eutaw Place Church, Mary Armstrong was already involved in foreign missions interests and prayer. In 1868 (when Annie was only 18) Mama's friend Ann Baker Graves was baptized at First Baptist Church in Baltimore and began to encourage women to organize for missions causes. Ann's son was Dr. Roswell Graves, one of the first missionary doctors. Roswell had gone to China at the age of 23 and ended up serving for more than fifty years. Roswell wrote to his mama about the needs of China's women. They needed to hear about Jesus, just like the men did. He urged Mrs. Graves to organize women to pray for China and to send money to support a Chinese Bible woman who could go into homes where the ladies lived and tell them about Jesus' love for them. (Her job would be to reach women who never came to church. This Bible woman would take the good news to them personally.)

Ann Graves was a brilliant and loving leader. Sure enough, one of the first to join Mrs. Graves' group was Mary Armstrong. In May 1868, when the Southern Baptist Convention met in Baltimore, Ann gathered women together for their own meeting. Those women prayed for missionaries and for the millions of people who had never heard about God's love. The ladies prayed to find ways they could personally help. Soon, Eutaw Place Church had its own Woman's Mission to Woman group. Annie and Alice's mama was an officer in this first society.

One of Annie's favorite projects became the ever-present mite box. Each member of the society had a little garnet-colored box. The Armstrongs placed their three little boxes on the dining table. Every week, each of them would put two pennies in her mite box. It seemed so little, but with everyone in the society doing their part, there was soon enough money for Dr. Graves to hire a Chinese Bible woman to go into the homes in Canton, China, and share the story of God's love. Annie loved having a tangible way to feel like she was helping share Jesus' story on the other side of the world. Just pennies — but pennies working together did a lot.

Soon the Armstrongs felt a *direct* link to missions in China. Annie would never forget her surprise when their good friend, Jane Norris, took them aside one Sunday morning after church. It was 1872, a brand-new year, and morning services had just ended.

"Annie and Alice," Jane smiled, her eyes sparkling, "I have some news."

Annie and Alice waited impatiently, "Yes, Jane? Tell us!"

After a suspenseful pause, Jane announced. "I'm going to China."

Annie and Alice spoke on the same breath, "You are *what*? What in the world?"

"You know," Jane explained, excitement filling her voice, "Dr. Graves is in Baltimore just now, back from China. Well," Jane paused for breath, "he has asked me to marry him, and return to China with him as a missionary!"

Annie, the more impetuous of the sisters, gave Jane a huge hug. "Oh Jane, how romantic!"

All of them laughed at Annie's reaction. It was so unlike the usually matter-of-fact, always practical, Annie Armstrong to call something "romantic." The three excitedly began to talk about wedding plans.

"Jane, I feel like part of our family is now going to be thousands of miles away doing God's work." Annie declared. "This makes missions seem so personal."

So it was that in April, Eutaw Place Church had a dedication service for Dr. Graves and his new wife, Jane, and six other missionaries on their way to China. Annie and Alice were thrilled to be at the service and feel a part of what God was going to be doing in China. Their pennies in the mite boxes were going to be very busy.

Annie knew missions work on the other side of the world was really important. But then, it was also important that they help people in America know about God. Annie often thought, *How can it be, in this land with all its freedom and promise, that so many people don't know a thing about the Heavenly Father?* Annie thought about the immigrants from around the world who arrived in Baltimore Harbor every week. *Who will share the good news with them?* This question lingered in Annie's mind and wouldn't go away.

Meanwhile, another need caught Annie's attention in a big way. She and Alice were invited to attend a meeting at First Baptist Church and hear a brilliant speaker. Mrs. Quinton was from Philadelphia and was president of the National Indian Association. (In those days, Native-born Americans, or those who were indigenous, were known as Indians.) The Armstrong sisters thought about the needs of these people who had called America "home" for thousands of years. Many of the tribes had been mistreated by settlers who came from Europe to make America their home. Now these indigenous people were being forced out — herded from their homes and moved to the Southwest to live on the great plains. Annie and Alice were shocked. Soon, the young women of Eutaw Place Church banded together and organized a home mission society to help. Not surprisingly, those women quickly elected Annie Armstrong as their president. Annie always seemed full of new and helpful ideas. (This happened before WMU organized and was moving in the direction of women working together in missions.)

Some years earlier, Annie's Uncle Eugene Levering had died and left a legacy of $2,500 to the Home Mission Board of the Southern Baptist Convention. Now, about the time Annie and Alice and church friends had organized the new women's home mission society, Baptists had used Levering's money to build an industrial school in Wetumka, Oklahoma. It was right at the center of the Creek Nation in what was called Indian Territory. The Home Mission Board in Atlanta heard about Annie and this new group that was interested in helping the Indians. Almost immediately, Annie's group was asked to be an auxiliary of the Board. Annie and Alice both felt the excitement of this new challenge — Alice in her quiet way, and Annie with her usual take-charge, energetic fashion.

The spring of 1881 found the new Levering school in Oklahoma in a tough situation. The local government had failed to give their promised portion of expenses, and the school needed practical help — and fast. A plea came from the Home Mission Board. *Could the women of Baltimore possibly make two sets of clothing for each student? And by the way, there are 120 of them!*

Upon receiving the news, Annie called a meeting of their society. "Ladies, we must do something," she spoke as she presented the problem to the young women. "We need 240 sets of clothing, of suits, and," and she paused and looked around at their group, "there is not enough time to make that many suits between now and summer when they are desperately needed." Heads around the room nodded in agreement.

Quickly, the ladies divided up and visited the other churches in their city. Sure enough, Baptist women of all ages, and from all across Baltimore, were soon cutting, measuring, fitting and completing a high stack of clothing. As suits were finished, they were packed in barrels and prayed over. Soon, barrels full of clothing were on the way to Oklahoma in time for summer. And behind them was a large group of Baptist women who had found a practical way to make a difference in the lives of young indigenous students in a territory out on the great plains.

Not only the women of Baltimore, but also the leadership of the Home Mission Board, noted the talent and leadership skills of young Miss Annie Armstrong. In that same year, Annie was asked to be president of the newly organized Home Mission Society of Maryland. (She served as their leader many years, along with scores of other jobs she took on.)

These were busy and exciting years for young Annie. And always at her side, supporting, encouraging, and helping her, was her sister Alice. Sometimes at night, after an exhausting day, the two would arrive home and collapse into easy chairs.

"Alice," Annie would frequently say, "I could never do all this without you. You are indispensable, and don't you ever forget it!"

Alice often replied with a sigh, "Annie, I am also exhausted. Aren't you too? Where does all your energy come from?"

The year 1881 was unusual in a very different way for Annie. She was increasingly busy with her teaching at church and working in the asylum, the orphanage and the mission society. Then in addition, something completely unexpected happened in her personal life. She received a proposal of marriage. It took her completely by surprise. She had enjoyed teasing their friend, Jane Norris, about being a "romantic"

A Fresh Beginning: 1873–1881   29

years earlier, but she would never have described herself with that word.

Annie had often pondered what God wanted her to do with her life. Often at night, when she and Alice talked over a day's activities, Annie would sigh and say, "Alice, sometimes I'm just not sure what God wants me to do. I want to do what He has in mind, but I just don't know what that might be."

Alice, in her usual quiet way, would respond with reassuring words, "Why, Annie, I know the Lord will surely show you His plans for you."

One night, Annie looked puzzled as she said to Alice, "Sister, ever since Jane went to China, I have wondered if God wanted me to be a foreign missionary too. I really don't know. But," she sighed in resignation, "I do know one thing. I simply cannot learn a foreign language. Look what a mess I made of my foreign language classes during school. I love history, of course, and I love math. But I never *can* get the accents right on languages."

Alice gave her comforting smile and responded, "Sister, don't fret. When God calls you to something, He equips you to do that very thing. He knows your talents. After all," said Alice, "He gave you those skills!"

And the day came for 30-year-old Annie when she confronted this very question head on. That spring, a well-known missionary from China, quite a bit older than Annie, was visiting churches in Baltimore. His wife had died some time previously and he had four young children to care for. He was also eager to return to China to his work. Annie and Alice first met him at their church and then again at a dinner party in the city. And, surprisingly, the next time she was invited to dinner at her sister Mamie Levering's home, Dr. Jesse Hartwell was there again.

Her sister Mamie met Annie at the door, telling her with a grin, "Annie, Dr. Hartwell is here for dinner tonight. I think he is interested in you," she smiled broadly. "He certainly seems intrigued by my sister Annie." Annie felt a flush spread over her cheeks. "Mamie," and her eyes were wide as she protested, "I think you are joking." Mamie cocked her head to one side again and grinned as she replied, "Well-l-l-l," and she dragged the word out, "he pointedly asked me if you would be here tonight!"

Annie hardly had time to think about what Mamie had said before she was ushered into the dining room to join the other guests. Sure enough, Dr. Hartwell was there, and it was also clear that she was the focus of his attention. After the meal, Dr. Hartwell asked to speak to her in the parlor. Annie was in a state of shock as he got right to the point. He was so impressed, he told her, about what he had learned about her work, and how she led various groups and how she reached out to help the needy. Dr. Hartwell then spoke of his work in China and how he wanted to get back to it. He told her of his four young children who needed a mother. After a meaningful pause, he added, "Miss Annie, would you do me the honor of consenting to be my wife?"

Annie Armstrong was never at a loss for words. However, that night she came close. This distinguished, articulate man, was asking *her* to become his *wife*? In a state of shock, she stumbled a bit over her words as she responded, "Sir, I, uh, I am honored that you would ask me such a question. Please, though, I … I need a bit of time."

Dr Hartwell was gracious, "Of course you do. You can let me know whenever you wish. I am in the city for several weeks."

Annie went home in something of a daze. Her mind was in a state of unusual confusion. This was a huge decision. For days, she pondered. She prayed. She talked with Sister. Alice always helped to soothe her and to help her think straight. She talked with Mama. And she prayed again. And again. Above all, she wanted to do the right thing. She wanted to do what God wanted. At long last, Annie had the right answer. She was honored, but she knew in her heart that this was not God's leading for her. And she now felt with certainty that God *did* have a special ministry for her. It felt like one door was closing and another one was opening. She was to do God's work right here in America. She just needed to find out what that was.

The Rest of the Story

Just think: If Annie Armstrong had accepted Dr. Hartwell's marriage proposal, she would have lived and worked in the same area in China as did Lottie Moon — coworkers on the field! As it was, they were *indeed* coworkers in women's work — Annie on this side of the world, Lottie on the other. It was Lottie Moon, more than any other single influence, who urged and nudged and prayed Woman's Missionary Union into organizing in 1888. Lottie, the great letter writer, wrote many letters to pastors, to women leaders in America, and, most importantly, to Annie Armstrong and those involved in planning WMU into life. Lottie wrote urging them to work together. "Just look at the Methodist women," she pleaded, "They work together and look at how they are organized to do missions. Now look at the Presbyterian women. They are organized and can do much more because they are united in their work."

That tiny little lady thousands of miles away in China prayed and urged the Baptist women in the Southern United States to do the same. And the chief agent of that change would be a young woman about ten years younger than Lottie Moon. The call would soon come, and Annie Armstrong would answer it.

View of Baltimore in the 1850s.
(Courtesy of National Woman's Missionary Union)

Early mite box (Courtesy of Woman's Missionary Union Archives, Birmingham, Alabama)

Chapter Four

SOMETHING NEW
1882–1887

Annie hurried into the living room with the day's mail. She smiled big as she waved a letter she had just opened.

"Listen to this," she called out to Mama and Alice. "This is a letter from the Levering School in Oklahoma Territory. They are telling us how deeply they appreciate all the suits we made. Because of our help, they say, 'disaster is avoided and the school is going to survive' — hooray!" she breathlessly finished. The three Armstrongs were thrilled at the success of their first project to help home missions, and of course, Annie was busy thinking up ways to do even more.

Ever eager for a new challenge, Annie quickly told all of the women who had helped with the project about its success. "It was all because we worked together," she assured the ladies at their next meeting. "Our watchword, 'Our land for Christ,' is a noble one. Let's organize and see how we can make a difference," she explained. Annie was thrilled to see the enthusiasm of the group. Even younger women wanted to join the group.

Annie woke up on May 16 thinking, *Today is when everyone's coming to Eutaw Place!* Thrilled with excitement at breakfast, she asked Alice, "Sister, do you think we might be able to officially organize?" Alice smiled because Annie was being Annie, always eager for action. The sisters got to the church early, for they were the hosts for the gathering of women from all over Baltimore and beyond. Most of those entering the room were younger women. A few came out of curiosity, but many had helped with the suits for children in the school. They were eager to learn how to be active and do more. Before the afternoon was over, the ladies voted to organize and be known as the Woman's Baptist Home Mission Society of Maryland. A lady from First Baptist spoke up, "I'd like to nominate Miss Annie Armstrong to be our president." The only one who seemed surprised at the unanimous vote was Annie herself. She drew a deep breath and vowed in her heart to do the best she could to be the best leader she could be.

Summer was upon them. Ever since Annie was a little girl, the Armstrongs went to the mountains each summer for cool weather and relaxation. This year, as Annie was packing her bags for their usual trip, she stopped, put her hands on her hips, and shook her head.

"I just can't go," she declared.

"What?" Alice, who was packing her own bags, looked up in surprise. "What are you talking about?"

"Sister," Annie exclaimed, "I can't go with you and Mama this summer. I must visit churches in Maryland and get the women to organize. We need *all* of us working together!"

Alice shook her head, "But we always go to Virginia. Annie," she spoke matter-of-factly, "if you don't go, I won't either. I'll stay and visit these churches with you."

Annie shook her head, "Sister, Mama can't go on her own without one of us to help. Several of our friends at the church said they could go visit the churches also, so I won't be alone."

And go she did. Annie and three of her friends traveled by train and often by hired buggy. They sought out Baptist churches, one after another after another. Happily, most pastors were willing to gather the church women together to hear what "Miss Annie" had to say. The ladies listened, and then they organized. Immediately, she wrote Dr. Isaac Tichenor, the new head of the Home Mission Board, about Maryland women.

"Please," Annie wrote, "we want to help the board." He was thrilled and answered her immediately. Dr. Tichenor's letter was full of special ideas and ways the new organization could help. Mama and Alice came home from the mountains to find a happy and busy Annie waiting for them.

"Mama, Alice," there was excitement in Annie's voice, "we visited in a lot of small churches. And," she gave a long pause, "all except one of them have organized into a society!"

"Oh, Annie," Mary exclaimed, "it sounds like you sacrificing your summer vacation paid off in a special way!"

Annie grinned and added, "Plus, Mama, we have been gathering the children together and they are forming groups we are going to call Little Gleaners. Sister," she turned to look at Alice, "we need to prepare material for learning about all the missions needs. So," she grinned and her eyes twinkled, "we need your capable pen!"

Alice, who loved to write, quickly agreed, and right away, she and Annie began preparing material for Little Gleaners each month.

Every day was a busy day at the Armstrong home. The Maryland Woman's Home Mission Society grew and began helping the many immigrant groups in Baltimore. There seemed to be a new need and project every month. Annie loved nothing better than to organize and challenge others. Her mind was always busy thinking up new ideas.

Suddenly, it was 1884, and here came a new opportunity for missions. Little did Annie realize that this was the beginning of a special task God had in mind for her. At breakfast one February morning, Mary Armstrong reminded her daughters, "Girls, you remember back in '68, when Mrs. Graves invited all the Baptist women to a meeting when the Southern Baptist Convention met here in Baltimore?" Both sisters nodded.

"Certainly, Mama, that was an exciting time," Annie spoke up.

"Well," Mary's eyes sparkled, "the convention is meeting here in Baltimore again this year. And I want us to help welcome all these women back to our city. Baltimore is where we meet again this year. I hope and pray we can have this kind of gathering *every* year at convention time," Mary concluded.

Annie, her mind already at work on new ideas, added to her mother's thoughts, suggesting, "Let's start thinking about making these annual meetings official. "Look," Annie looked directly into the eyes of both her mother and her sister as she proposed, "we know that other states have societies like ours. Why can't we think about organizing and working together?" Annie leaned back in her chair, gave an emphatic nod of her head and declared, "We would be a lot stronger and get a lot more done if we worked together. Let's don't just stand *still*. I think we need to go forward!" she finished with a flourish.

Mary Armstrong was as excited as her two daughters. "Girls," she added, "I don't think we are the only ones wanting to organize. I just learned at our Woman to Woman meeting this week that our society is now the central committee for woman's work in Maryland. Every state," she explained, "has a central committee. You remember the convention

Something New: 1882–1887

last year was in Waco, Texas." Both daughters nodded, "Well, they are suggesting that every state have someone from their central committee get together at our next meeting."

Annie spoke up, "Mama, that will be our meeting here in Baltimore in May!" Her voice was bright with excitement. Mary smiled as she answered, "Yes indeed. And just think, the three of us will be part of this new direction."

Annie was impatient for May to arrive. The feeling as the women began filing into the meeting at Seventh Place Baptist Church was one of anticipation. Annie and Alice felt it from the very beginning. How special that this meeting was in the very place where, in 1868, Ann Baker Graves had first invited women to gather to pray for missions and specifically for her son, Dr. Graves, in South China. Sixteen years had passed, and women were finally getting near to a national organization. As president of Maryland's Home Mission Society, Annie was flushed with excitement to think about this important step forward. She and Alice realized there were even four or five women here today that had been present that first time in May 1868.

The moment came for the reading of the resolution to begin organizing, and Annie leaned forward in her pew to catch every word. The proposal was to meet every year when the Convention met and have the central committees from each state be responsible for plans. Annie's mind was racing. She thought, *Lord, this is really happening. Let this be for Your glory.* There was a feeling of expectancy in the Armstrong household as they thought about what might be the next step. Soon enough, however, came news that even wonderful things sometimes have roadblocks standing in the way.

The Leverings and Armstrongs were a family of believers who loved each other and their church. The Levering men were quite unusual for men of their time. Many men in the 1800s felt like women should be helpers and not leaders. Somehow the average man in many churches felt like only men should talk and be in charge. They felt threatened that women would want to "take over." But not the Levering men. They felt like God worked in the hearts of all His children, and they welcomed women helping and being involved.

Annie's earlier church had been very much controlled by men. That wasn't true at Eutaw Place Church, and Annie loved the freedom of being able to help in all the ways that she felt God leading her. However, Annie did grow up with the conviction that it was not good for women to speak in a meeting where men were also present. This feeling followed her all her life, and it made for some difficult situations when she later became a national leader.

The idea of women in leadership was a problem sitting there facing Baptist women. However, they refused to allow it to discourage them. *God is going to make a way,* Annie thought. *God understands that we don't want to control — but just to help. Let us just see what He will do.* Baptist women rejoiced, the Armstrong ladies included, when Dr. Henry Tupper became director of the Foreign Mission Board. He was a big supporter of women in missions. He was excited to think of what God might do through women in missions efforts. Why, even having the central committee from each state was his idea, and he was constantly writing letters and encouraging the women's work. Here was a man who recognized how important women were to missions.

"Look at this, Alice!" and Annie held out the copy of the Baltimore Baptist paper, pointing to a column on the front page. "This article has your name written all over it." She finished with a flourish.

Puzzled, Alice reached out and took the paper. "What are you talking about, Sister?" she asked as she read the article.

"Just read that paragraph, Alice," Annie insisted. "It says the *Baltimore Baptist* paper is asking the home and foreign missions societies to encourage women to subscribe to their paper, and," she spoke with satisfaction, "they are going to give women a regular column in the *Baltimore Baptist!* That means you — my dear sister — you can be editor for the home missions column!"

Alice couldn't keep a smile off her face. "Oh, Annie, you know me so well — I love to write. This seems like a perfect way to get missions knowledge out there for the children and the grown-ups too." Alice knew that her sister was the organizer, while she loved to have a pen in her hand and write the story of God at work. And in no time at all, "Aunt Addie's" column was in the paper each edition, and children all over Maryland were learning exciting stories about what God was doing for children and adults too.

Annie and Alice officially joined the foreign society where their mama was so active. Both the home and foreign societies would write for the missions column in each issue of the paper. And right on the heels of this new beginning, Annie got involved in her biggest project ever. Baptist men in the state realized that in order to get people involved in missions efforts, everyone needed to understand what the needs were. Baptists needed missions reading material. Leaders decided to start a committee to set up a missions library and reading rooms. And, wonder of wonders, those men wanted women on the planning committee!On the evenings when Annie and Alice did not have one meeting or another, they often talked through plans for literature.

"Sister," it was like Annie was thinking aloud, "we have new societies springing up all over the state. You know," she stopped and raised her hand to emphasize the point, "they have to have missions material. They have to know what to *pray* for."

Alice gave a bit of a smile and finished the thought, "Yes, Sister, someone has to prepare all of this material. And you know," she shook her head, "there are just two of us."

Annie grinned and explained, "But Alice, we have pastors here in Baltimore, like our own Dr. Fuller, who will also write. And I'll prepare some prayer cards." Within the year, Maryland Baptists started a missions reading room in Baltimore. Who was heading it up? Annie Armstrong. Annie's creative brain kept thinking of new ideas. Foreign missions leaflets, home missions leaflets, all sorts of reading material, was prepared. People in Baltimore could come in and read missions news, and people all over America could order mission stories and information. Annie developed a catalog so Baptists anywhere could order the material they needed.

Summer came, and again Annie insisted, "I just don't have time to go with our family and sister Mamie and her children to Virginia, to the mountains." She had not counted on how stubborn and persuasive her family could be.

"Annie," her cousin Josh insisted, "that's simple. Pack your work material, and then you can breathe in the cool, clean mountain air and work at the same time!"

So, that was just what Annie did. One day in Virginia, while Annie and Alice were strolling and enjoying the scenery, a gentleman recognized them and introduced himself.

"I am Mr. Dickinson, editor of the Baptist paper of Virginia, the *Baptist Herald*." He gave a little bow and smile, and continued, "I have heard about the fine work you are beginning with Baptist missions literature in Maryland. And," he added, "Miss Alice, I am impressed with your writing as 'Miss Addie.' Would you also please write a column in our state paper here in Virginia?" Mr. Dickinson was well aware of the problem women were having about promoting missions when many of the pastors objected to women taking any role in leadership. He wanted women to have an opportunity to contribute their ideas just as did the men. Alice paused for a long time, and then accepted, with the understanding that she could write under a "pen" name, not her own. And with that, the name of Ruth Alleyn (Alice Armstrong) became a very familiar one to women in many states."Aunt Addie" and "Ruth Alleyn," a.k.a. Alice Armstrong, was right there assisting Annie in all her hard work. It was an exciting day when Annie handed Alice a folder. Alice looked at it and exclaimed, "Sister, you have the catalog ready!"

Annie gave a big smile, "Just think, tracts and leaflets and prayer cards can be ordered by Baptist women all over America. Now," she sighed with satisfaction, "They will have material to guide their meetings."

Often at night, the sisters would walk wearily home from the reading room. After one particularly long day, Annie sighed and remarked, "Alice, I could never do all this without you. You are better than an extra right hand. And you are such a help with our volunteers who come each day."

Alice laughed and suggested, "I guess we can be called the team of AA and AA." (For many years, Annie Armstrong headed the well-known reading room. In fact, in addition to all her other jobs, she remained as head of the Baltimore reading room until the time a WMU magazine was produced.)

Annie's brain never seemed to rest. Whether sitting at her desk in the reading room at 10 East Fayette Street in downtown Baltimore, or at her desk at home, Annie's mind was constantly churning. She would think through the day's work. She would ponder what could be done better. She would speculate on how to involve more people. Sometimes she simply tried to figure out how to get all the meetings, errands, writing, and work fitted in to a single day. There were never enough hours. Sometimes, she would pray, *Lord, I need direction. I want to use my time in a way that honors You.*

God did show her. That spring of 1887, Annie's ever-active mind was getting excited about what might happen at their next woman's annual meeting in Louisville, Kentucky. But not even the keen mind of Annie could imagine all that God had in store for her.

The Rest of the Story

There are many unanswered questions about Annie Armstrong and how and why she developed into the strong leader she became. Not a great deal was recorded. No one knows the different private schools she attended, only that she had a finely trained mind. Annie loved music and often enjoyed leading singing. Where did the musical influence in her life come from? It is also something of a mystery that Annie was always firm about never speaking to an audience that included men. Why? Could it be that, because at Seventh Baptist Church, her early church, all the leaders were men? On the other hand, it is well-known that at Eutaw Place Church, many women were in leadership. That was Annie's home church for the remainder of her life. Furthermore, from the time she was a young girl, Annie had always wanted to be in business, just like a man could work in a business. That makes her determination not to speak to an audience that included men a bit of a mystery. We may never know the answer.

Home of the Friendless, where Annie volunteered for many years. (Courtesy of National Woman's Missionary Union)

Annie Armstrong's desk, where she spent many hours. (Courtesy of National Woman's Missionary Union)

Chapter Five

Go Forward!
1887–1888

The evening train for Baltimore pulled out of Louisville's main depot, and three women sank back on their comfortable red velour cushioned seats. The oldest of the three, small and noticeably tired, leaned back on the headrest with a satisfied sigh. Mary Armstrong gazed at her two daughters, both extremely tall and seated like loving guards, one on each side of her.

"Girls," she asked, "are you happy with the way our meeting went?" Both "girls" grinned, making them look years younger than their actual 42 and 38 years. The younger reached out to pat her mother's small hand.

"Oh, yes, Mama," Annie had a twinkle in her eyes. "It *more* than exceeded my expectations."

Her mother responded, "Wonderful. I was afraid you might be upset that we didn't officially organize this year, after all your work and effort."

"Absolutely not," Annie spoke quickly, and Alice nodded in agreement. "This meeting was so good. We spent so much time and effort during the year laying a foundation. There are more and more women now who understand and are eager to actually take the next step and organize. They don't feel rushed.

"You see, Mama," Annie spoke earnestly, "many of the women live in states where a lot of men are outspoken in their fear that women will want to 'take over.' Now these ladies feel confident to go back to their states and explain that we women only want to organize to be efficient and raise funds for missions."

Alice quickly added, "I think one reason they have asked Annie to head up the planning now is because of the Baptist men in leadership in Maryland. They support us and work *with* us." She gave a little chuckle, "I think those ladies hope that the men in their *own* states might catch a little bit of that attitude!"

Annie gave a rather undignified snort and tossed her head, "Yes, I even heard a Baptist pastor from one of those states comment that 'these women are going to break up our churches.' The very idea! We simply want to *help*." Annie finished in a voice filled with determination, "And, we women will make an amazing contribution. You just wait and see!"

Annie and Alice had already spent many hours in planning ahead. Thanks to them, the women of the convention now had a plan, and 'a plan to *work* the plan,' as Annie liked to say. Dr. Tupper, who headed the Foreign Mission Board, was behind them 100 percent, and he was a great ally.

"Just think," Annie was enthusiastic, "we have agreed that each state will work on ideas and plans and bring them as resolutions to our meeting next year in Richmond. And, Sister," she looked at Alice, "your writing is so persuasive! Most of the women do not know who 'Ruth Alleyn' is. You, writing as Ruth Alleyn, have influenced them. Now they understand why women are so important to the work of missions." She finished on a satisfied sigh, "I am really glad Mr. Dickinson in Virginia asked you to write that monthly women's column in their state paper. It gives Baptist women a voice! And, Alice," she reached over and patted Alice's knee to emphasize her point, "I am so glad you have an amazing pen. It is a God-given talent."

Mary Armstrong was beaming. "Girls," she smiled that sweet smile that always melted their hearts, "I am so thankful for you. Alice, your talent in writing, and Annie, your leadership abilities." Then she added, "I saw the way the ladies from the various states kept looking at you. You have become quite well-known."

Annie looked puzzled. "But, Mama, why would they look at *me*? Or know who I am? I was just one of the delegates."

Mary shook her head, "Annie, don't you realize that your name is very familiar to women now? You have been mailing out thousands of leaflets of missions information and prayer cards to women all over the South. And our Baltimore missions reading room is becoming so important. Also, Annie," Mary finished on a chuckle, "you pretty well stand out in a crowd, you know. All six feet of you!"

The Armstrongs returned to Baltimore, but not to rest up from the trip. Alice was not surprised that her younger sister went to work immediately on planning for the big meeting next year. Sometimes Alice wondered if Annie worked on just half a night's sleep. She never seemed to slow down. All their lives, Mary Armstrong had trained her children to think for themselves. Now it seemed like Annie couldn't *stop* thinking. It concerned Alice that her sister didn't get enough rest. She was constantly at her desk writing and planning. If not writing, she was up and going to yet another meeting.

It was soon time for the Armstrong ladies to head to the Virginia mountains for their summer vacation. All three went, but Annie was loaded down with all sorts of missions pamphlets and material to distribute. She also took boxes of material to aid in working on plans to organize. Alice took her "creative pen" as Annie called her sister's ability to write well and persuasively. "Ruth Alleyn," the name she used on her articles, had become quite well-known. Mr. Dickinson, the editor of Virginia Baptists' influential paper, gave her high praise in an article that came out just before the women gathered in 1888 in Richmond. He wrote, "Ruth Alleyn Again! Weighty Words from a Wise Woman." He praised the plans of Baptist women to organize.

Annie and Alice worked constantly in the months leading up to the May meeting of women in Richmond. Annie was writing letters every day to leaders of central committees (the women who led in each state). Careful plans for their upcoming Richmond meeting needed to be worked out. Large on everyone's mind was the need for a strong and worthy constitution to guide them. Annie was especially ashamed when she realized that Baptist women had given *less* to missions this past year than they had three years earlier. She felt even worse when she read how much Methodist and Presbyterian women had given. It was far more than Baptists. Annie thought, *Is that not proof yet again that we Baptists need to organize and work together? We can do so much more that way.*

The closer the time got to May and the annual meeting, the more excited Annie became. *Dear Lord,* she prayed each day, *please give us the wisdom we don't have, and help us organize to serve you better.* Annie came to know several state leaders quite well and they passed letters and ideas back and forth every week. (Little could Annie have known how many thousands of letters she would be writing in the years just ahead.) She especially admired Martha ("Mattie") McIntosh from South Carolina. Mattie was chair of the central committee there and worked tirelessly to bring women and ideas together. She was neither forceful nor pushy. Instead, Mattie was both quiet and dignified, but her calm manner and soft southern accent could fool a person into thinking she was meek and mild. Not so. That ladylike manner hid an exceptionally keen mind and wise heart.

Annie was also very impressed with Eliza Broadus. Her father was president of Southern Baptist Theological Seminary and a well-known Baptist leader. Eliza was passionate about missions. She worked tirelessly. Of course, Annie herself, who never slept for long periods, knew about working nonstop. Annie and Eliza had a lot in common. Then there was Fannie Davis from Texas. She was another keen leader, and Annie liked the way she got things done.

Early on the morning of May 11, Annie's eyes popped open. She instantly recalled they were in Richmond, and today was the opening of the meeting. Immediately, the excitement of the moment brought her wide awake. At last! After all these years, the day had finally come — the day to organize. This was no sure thing, of course. But to Annie's way of thinking, it was going to be now or never. The plans were deep and well-considered.

Annie stood in front of the bureau mirror automatically braiding her long brown hair into its customary braids piled high on her head with a hair comb. She could braid it without looking. Next came her crisp new black silk dress with her favorite cameo at the high-collared throat. Annie smiled as she pinned her lapel watch on the front of her dress. *Yes, here was time — and this was surely the time for Baptist women.*

The large basement Sunday school room of Broad Street Methodist

Church in Richmond was milling with Baptist women when the Armstrongs arrived. *There must be at least 200 here*, Annie thought. She could feel expectancy hanging in the air. Twelve of the states had sent delegates — and that meant more than thirty official voting delegates. Even more states were represented by interested ladies. Annie looked around eagerly. Yes, Mattie McIntosh was in earnest conversation with a lady from Missouri. Fannie Breedlove, all the way from Texas, was gesturing as she talked with Eliza Broadus. Among the new faces was lovely young Fannie Heck from North Carolina. She was just in her mid-twenties, but Annie knew she was already a strong leader in her state. Annie's heart gave a little leap to think of so many strong, capable, and dedicated women in one place — all with the same goal in mind.

Each state had three official delegates, and everyone was free to comment and make suggestions. Annie smiled to see two adorable girls who had come along with their mother, Abby Gwathmey of Virginia. That mother of nine wanted to be sure her 11-year-old twins were present to observe what promised to be an historic moment for Baptist women. Annie was especially pleased that their own pastor, Dr. Ellis from Baltimore, was bringing the opening devotional. He was brief but also encouraging in what he said. He was 100 percent behind women organizing for missions and not wasting time. He concluded by challenging them, "If you know what to do, go ahead and do it! If not, take more time. However, *more* time is *losing* time." And, with a smile of encouragement, Dr. Ellis left for the Southern Baptist Convention meeting nearby.

Annie listened intently as Eliza Stout of South Carolina read a paper she had written, persuasively outlining *why* women needed to organize. Annie sat there, inwardly saying, *Yes, yes, that is what we need to do!* When Eliza finished speaking, Alice Armstrong read a strong paper about the importance of women forming a union. Then Annie rose to her feet. Of course, her regal height drew all eyes. In a forceful voice that commanded attention, she spoke, "I request that a resolution for organization be considered immediately, followed by a free exchange of ideas." Fannie Breedlove, after traveling four long days by train to get to Richmond, quickly rose to second Annie's motion. Many suggestions were offered from nearly every state. Some were eager to go on and vote. Others wanted to wait.

Annie breathed a sigh of relief when it was voted to have one delegate from each state meet over the weekend and draw up plans (and a constitution) for the new organization she and Alice had dreamed of for so long. To no one's surprise, Annie was the delegate from Maryland for the committee. She was prepared. Alice and Annie had spent many hours studying constitutions for all sorts of church organizations. Annie had consulted with their cousin, Josh Levering, who was president of the Southern Baptist Convention. A prominent Baptist lawyer had also been very helpful. All weekend, Annie and the committee worked on details. She could scarcely wait until Monday. It felt like women were finally ready to meet history face to face.

Alice noticed a spring in her sister's step as they headed to the Monday morning meeting. Breathing in the crisp May air, Annie gave a quick glance at Alice's face and confessed, "Sister, I didn't sleep a whole lot last night. I was too excited."

Alice nodded in understanding, "I'll admit I was restless too. Just think of all these years of praying, planning, working. This may be the day."

Annie smiled, "Alice, I think you have the right of it."

Resolution was written all over Annie Armstrong's face as they entered Broad Street Church. A rustle of skirts filled the air as more than 200 Baptist women sat down to see history being made. Annie listened with rapt attention as her friend Mattie McIntosh read the proposed constitution their committee had prepared over the weekend.

Finally, a call for a vote was made. Ten of the fourteen states voted to organize now. Annie felt like she was sitting in the middle of history. She literally had chill bumps. The vote was complete. They were a union!

The name of this new union was long. It was the Executive Committee of the Woman's Mission Societies, Southern Baptist Convention (now known as Woman's Missionary Union). It was a long name, and they had a big job to do. Immediately, the new organization went to work. The first order of business was a location for headquarters. One delegate rose to state that all of them knew Maryland was a leader in new beginnings. Furthermore, Maryland women had the support of pastors in their state. She moved that Baltimore be the new headquarters. Fannie Breedlove from Texas quickly seconded the motion. Annie suddenly found things moving fast for a change. It felt good. She liked fast.

Now Annie stood, cleared her throat, and stated, "Ladies, if Baltimore is to be our union's headquarters, we need a president from another part of the Southern Baptist Convention. I propose," she concluded on a deep breath, "that South Carolina shall furnish a president in the person of Miss McIntosh." A murmur of approval rippled across the large room as Mattie was enthusiastically elected as WMU's first president. Mattie then rose to preside over business.

Mattie had everyone's attention as she stated, "We need to select our officers today. The great amount of work will fall to our executive committee. This group will determine the success of all we have done. Above all," she continued, "we need a strong corresponding secretary to lead. It is our most important post."

Suddenly, Annie could sense eyes looking at her. She quickly glanced around and realized everyone was looking straight at her. A sudden and strange feeling of inevitability flooded through Annie's body. She could not even see where the voice came from, but she heard someone say, "I nominate Annie Armstrong as our corresponding secretary." It flashed through her mind, *God, is this what you have been leading me to all these years?* Another voice called out, "I second the motion." And, before she knew it, Annie Armstrong was the leader of the newly formed Woman's Mission Societies of the Southern Baptist Convention. She felt excited. She felt unworthy. She felt overwhelmed. And, on the heels of these sensations, she remembered the Scripture, "Trust in the Lord with all your heart and lean not unto your own understanding. In all your ways acknowledge Him and He will direct your path." Annie vowed in that moment: *Yes, Lord. I trust You.* A new beginning was right around the corner — and a whole new world of responsibility and challenge.

The Rest of the Story

That day of May 14, 1888, Annie Armstrong did not know that for the next eighteen years of her life, she would gallantly and successfully shepherd a brand-new organization of women through untested and sometimes unfriendly waters. (Nor could she know that WMU would one day become the largest missions organization for women in the world.)

Women understood that many pastors feared women would want to dominate and lead everything. It took diplomacy and ingenuity and prayer to convince many leaders of the SBC that women were coming alongside. They wanted to support and strengthen the work of the whole denomination. Women didn't want control, or to boss others around. They simply wanted to do their part in learning about missions, praying for missions, giving to missions, doing missions and participating in the work of the church. (GAs, young and old, does that sound a bit familiar?) We have been doing that for more than 130 years and counting. Annie's favorite phrase has become the true motto of Girls in Action. (These two small words held a world full of meaning: GO

— always means action! FORWARD — we keep moving ahead in all we do.) Those are the same words Annie spoke to that historic group of women on May 14, 1888: GO FORWARD.

Eutaw Place Baptist Church, Annie's longtime church, of which she was a charter member. (Courtesy of National Woman's Missionary Union)

WMU's first headquarters, 10 East Fayette Street, Baltimore. (Courtesy of National Woman's Missionary Union)

Chapter Six

WMU Is Born
1888–1890

Annie glanced up at the sign hanging above the desk in her Baltimore office. It always brought a smile to her face — GO FORWARD. *Yes,* she thought, *that is what I pray all of us will do! There is so much to do.* This suited her perfectly — more to do than time to do it in. Anyone really acquainted with Annie Armstrong knew she never wasted time. These were thrilling days for a young woman who loved ideas and goals. Baptist women were now a union — Annie, the union leader, determined not to fail them.

Dr. Tichenor of the Home Mission Board already had a big project and wanted the women's help. He told Annie there were over 1,000 new believers in Havana, Cuba, and more than 2,000 eager children in Sunday school there. However, there was no church building in which to have Sunday school, worship, and grow. Dr. Tichenor asked Annie if WMU would help Baptists raise $50,000 for a church building in Havana, Cuba. Could women raise $5,000? That was a *lot* of money in 1888. Annie's creative mind went to work. She thought of "brick cards" (little boxes) in which to collect the money. WMU agreed to set a goal of $5,000 — and use the "brick cards" to collect the money. It didn't surprise Annie that when she sent out hundreds of letters to all the societies in churches — women responded, and the money was raised.

She next decided there needed to be a special project for foreign missions too. Annie visited the Foreign Mission Board in Richmond, Virginia. "Dr. Tupper," she asked the leader, "please tell us a real need in a foreign land. Our women want to get to work."

Dr. Tupper was excited and reached to a corner of his desk. Picking up a letter and handing it to Annie, he responded, "I think I have just the right thing for you." It was a letter from Lottie Moon.

Annie's eyes sparkled, "Our own dear Miss Moon," she exclaimed. "She has been wanting Baptist women to organize for missions for years!"

Lottie's letter captured Annie's mind and heart as she read. Miss Moon was pleading for money to send more missionaries. Lottie wrote that she was breaking down physically and badly needed a furlough. "But how can I leave?" Lottie explained. "There is no one to stand in the gap and do the work while I am away. Please," she begged, "start a missions offering at Christmas and raise enough money to send two more missionaries." ($2,000 was the amount she suggested.)

It was a wonderful letter. Lottie Moon, (just like Annie) wrote hundreds, even thousands of letters! This became the famous "Christmas letter" where Miss Moon pleaded with Baptists to take an offering at Christmas time, when people were in the "giving" mood. Lottie wrote, "I wonder how many of us really believe it is more blessed to give than to receive? How many are there among us who imagine that, because 'Jesus paid it all,' they need pay *nothing*?"

Annie realized that this could well have been her *own* situation, had she accepted that marriage proposal those many years ago. She, too, would have been in China and desperate for a rest. Annie was very moved by Lottie's plea. Returning to Baltimore, she immediately met with the WMU executive committee and then wrote all the state women leaders. Hundreds and hundreds of letters flowed from Annie's pen. Every night as the sisters walked home, Annie rubbed her hands. They were painfully sore. She was at her desk long hours every day, writing letter after letter. Thankfully, a faithful group of volunteers came to the office each day to address envelopes for all those letters and mail out countless packages of prayer cards and literature.

Annie wrote all the state leaders *and* more than 1,200 missionary societies. Women needed to know about Lottie's plea. Soon, Annie heard about a new invention — a typewriter that printed out alphabet letters on paper. Writing letters with a typewriter would be so much quicker. They were bound to be expensive, but Annie was determined to be more efficient. She must try to get one. There was important work to do, and a typewriter would save time.

Annie closely watched the results of the first two WMU missions projects. She was a great one for keeping track of information to help guide WMU work. She and her army of volunteers had sent out more than 11,000 brick cards for the Havana building project. Now it was time for the Week of Self-Denial and Prayer for Foreign Missions. Annie put her own offering for more missionaries to be sent to China in one of the more than 29,000 envelopes she and her team prepared. Annie's own Sunday school children each happily filled an offering envelope to join all the other envelopes.

The long hours and sore hands were worth the effort. Women and children caught the excitement. They gave. One morning, Annie received a letter from Mattie McIntosh, WMU president, with news about the offering. Annie jumped up from her desk and hurried into the next room where Alice was busy writing at her desk.

"Sister!" Alice could hear the excitement in Annie's voice. "It's a letter from Mattie — the offering is all in."

Annie's face was aglow, "Just think! Our women have given not just $2,000, but $3,315.26. It is enough for three new missionaries to go to China!" Two stately, dignified ladies suddenly acted like young girls, dancing for joy in the middle of the office. (Months later, Annie learned that when Lottie received the letter telling of the offering, she laid her head on her desk and wept with gratitude over God's answer to her prayers for help.)

Annie's first annual report to national WMU was full of joy at what God had done in just one year. But even as she thanked the women at the annual meeting in Fort Worth, Texas, for their wonderful efforts, she reminded them, "Ladies, in spite of all that we have done, just think: This giving comes to only an average of one nickel per Baptist lady to tell the whole world about God's love. We must let our motto guide all of us in the year ahead to truly Go Forward."

A few weeks later, Annie and Alice were eager to get home and tell their mother about the new assistant at their WMU headquarters. Annie was smiling broadly as she found her mother in her favorite rocking chair and reached down to warmly kiss her cheek.

"Mama," she sounded excited, "we have a brand-new assistant at the office and what a help it is! I am excited."

Mary was curious. "Who is she, Annie?"

Annie grinned, "Mama, she is an 'it.' We have one of the newfangled typewriters! Think how many more letters I can write every day! The typewriter is expensive, but it will be so worth it."

Alice joined in, "And now, Annie, your hand won't have to swell and throb with pain from trying to write so many letters by hand!" (Annie Armstrong's hands never quite recovered from the amazing number of letters she wrote. She always felt it was worth the effort, however.)

During the first year as leader of the new organization, Annie learned something about herself, something she had thought about since the time she was a young girl. One evening after the usual long day in the office, Annie had a chance to talk through the day with Mary Armstrong and Alice.

"Mama," she began, "do you recall when I was a young girl, and I thought it unfair that just because I was a girl, I couldn't be a business-woman someday?"

Mary nodded, "Oh, yes, Annie, and I agreed with you then. And," she smiled broadly, "I *still* agree. Look at you now!"

Annie's eyes filled with unusual tears and she nodded her head in amazement. "Mama, I was actually right. I love this job. My heart tells me this is what God has in mind for me just now."

As the three women sat talking, Annie added, "You know, I have had so many people, including the men who head up our boards, tell me I should accept a salary. I simply do not *feel* like I should. I know," she shook her head in emphasis, "for most people a salary is necessary. However, our living situation is such that I don't *have* to take a salary. I feel this is my stewardship to God. I want to do this as long as we are able."

Again, Annie's heart swelled with gratitude. She was blessed with a mother who cared and supported her, and with a sister who was like another pair of hands. Annie often felt like Alice was her "better self."

Sometimes, she would do something in haste or would unintentionally say something that hurt someone's feelings. She could take one look at Alice's face and see a look there that said, *No, Annie, try again.*

During those early years, Annie Armstrong learned just how busy a person could be. She needed to make dozens of speeches. She needed to make trips to other cities and states to help organize new societies. She needed to meet with board leaders. And, yes, she needed to write many letters to state leaders. Thankfully, mail service was quite reliable, and letters flew back and forth between Annie, board leaders, and hundreds of women.

One winter morning in 1890, Annie sat down at her desk and glanced around the busy office. *Have I really been in this job only two years? It seems like I've been doing this forever. And loving it.* Looking down at the pile of letters to be answered, her thoughts scrambled ahead, *I'm so glad I don't find all this correspondence and paperwork tiresome. And,* she got a quizzical look in her eyes, *it looks like I have gone from teenage years, when I pondered God's will for me, to actually putting* feet *to those thoughts. I wouldn't trade jobs with anyone!*

In front of her was a paper bearing two words — Frontier Boxes. The fascinating American frontier, with all those new and newly settled lands, intrigued Miss Annie's creative and brilliant mind. She recalled when she first learned of the indigenous people (then called Indians) who had been constantly pushed further and further west. What was life like for them? What would happen to them, with everyone taking over their land? The year of 1889 was the time of the great land rush with pioneers pushing into Oklahoma Territory.

This trend, combined with the words "Frontier Boxes," brought that vast area vividly into her mind. Years before, when she and women all over Baltimore had made clothing for the Levering School in Oklahoma Territory, Annie's mind had been captivated with indigenous people in

WMU Is Born: 1888–1890

the West. Also, hardy frontier missionaries out there lived on so little. The new frontier was primitive and life was a daily challenge. *How could they possibly survive?* It was a thought that never really left Annie. Often, the frontier would come to her mind and she would pray for a way to help. And, as she prayed, an idea began to form in Annie's mind. Sometimes her sister Alice thought she could nearly "see the wheels of a new plan turning in Annie's head."

One morning in early January, Alice brought an article to Annie for her to read and approve. She stopped and cocked her head to one side. "Annie," she began, "I can see some ideas rolling around in that creative head of yours. What are you thinking up now?"

Annie grinned, "Alice, you know me too well. Look at this letter I've just written to Dr. Tichenor at the Home Board."

Alice began reading, and exclaimed, "Oh, it's ideas for frontier boxes! Tell me more!"

Alice found a chair and sat down to hear what Annie was planning this time. "Well, I don't have to tell *you* what a frontier box is. You remember when we learned that the leader of missions work in Arkansas wrote about the destitute ministers in the frontier area?" Annie explained.

"Of course, I recall," Alice responded, "we were all shocked to hear how little they were living on, and wondered how they could possibly make it from day to day. And," she continued, "you and I and the executive committee talked it over and asked you, as our leader, to contact the board about us doing something."

Annie was nodding. "Yes, Sister," and she reached over to briefly pat Alice's hand, "and you know it is always my thinking that ideas are not simply *ours* as WMU women. We are organized to carry out the wishes of our mission boards." She paused, "Sister, just between you and me, I don't want *credit* for these visions and projects. I want the leaders of the boards to get the credit." The twinkle in her eyes was followed by the grin on her face, "You know, Alice, Baptists are going to accept the ideas more quickly if they come from the men!"

Alice looked quickly at the letter Annie handed her, "Wonderful news. Dr. Tichenor is coming to talk about WMU sending boxes all over the frontier to support the missionaries!"

And, within a couple of weeks, he was in the Baltimore office. The conditions frontier missionaries lived in were really bad: not enough food, clothing, shelter, education for their children.

"Dr. Tichenor," Annie assured him, "we women will do something about that. You just give us the names!"

That is exactly what happened. WMU women in all the states got information from their Baltimore headquarters: the names of frontier missionaries, ages of children, where they lived, what they needed. Each society chose a name and adopted a missionary family. They wrote and got sizes and ages. One family included Mrs. Lucy Stevens, 27 years old. She was 5-foot-3-inches tall, waist 25 inches, hips 36. Daughter Melly, 10, was 4-feet-8-inches tall. Each other child in the family was named and their ages listed. The information also included the frontier missionary father's name and description. Some of those families actually lived in a dugout or a cave because they had no money to rent a house. (When houses were available, they were only one-story because of the danger of cyclones.)

Annie made a silent vow that she was going to visit those frontier missionaries and help them realize they were not alone. WMU was their partner. (She kept that vow.) The first year the boxes began to arrive on the frontier was like Christmas. Women in the east lovingly sewed dresses for women and girls, and pants and shirts for boys and fathers. As they sewed, the women could just picture those children and parents. Some of the frontier children had never before had shoes or books of their own. Many young mothers cried with joy as the wooden crates were opened.

WMU Is Born: 1888–1890

They could *see* how God was providing for their personal needs. Sally, a little girl in frontier Arkansas, sat rocking her new rag doll for hours. It was the first baby doll she ever had.

Alice and Annie had a wonderful time helping their society at Eutaw Place Church sew and prepare their frontier box for a missionary family in Arkansas. Each society member made an outfit for one of the little children in a far-away frontier house or dugout. Sometimes Alice and Annie sewed far into the night. It was the only spare time they had. Along with their mother, they sewed and talked and wondered about the little children for whom they were sewing. It was one of the most personal and touching projects of their many years of helping others.

The beginning years of national Woman's Missionary Union were exciting. They were more than busy. They were a challenge. Annie discovered that leading and planning came naturally to her. She also realized that she usually felt her plan and idea about a new project was the correct one. It was hard to accept that she wasn't always right in her conclusions.

Often, at the end of a full day, the two sisters would talk the day over as they walked home. Quite often, Alice would find a tactful way to gently say, "Annie, it might have been wise if you had listened to Mrs. Brown. Her thoughts had some value to them." Then Annie might respond, "Oh, but Alice, I have seen this kind of thing before and know exactly how it should be planned. But," and she made a grimace of a smile, "I shouldn't have lost my temper like I did. I regret that."

Alice gave a dry chuckle and remarked, "Sister, do you ever think about the consequences of your words before you say them?"

Annie paused a long moment before drawing a long breath. "Alright, Alice, I must admit I was too hasty." However, just under her breath, Alice heard Annie mutter, "But I was right!"

Annie was beyond excited about the way women in all the states took part and began sending several hundred missionary boxes to the frontier. Even on the train back to Baltimore from the 1890 annual meeting in Fort Worth, when women first voted to take on the project, Annie had a lady from Alabama come to her train car. She tapped Annie on the shoulder, and said, "Miss Armstrong?" She had a deep and charming Southern accent. "I'm Annie too!" The young lady introduced herself as Annie Grace Tartt of Alabama. "Can you possibly supply me with the name of a frontier missionary right *now*? I want our society to get started on a frontier box immediately!" Sure enough, she returned to her church in Alabama with the name of a needy frontier family in Oklahoma.

Frontier boxes were exciting hands-on missions, but each day always held a new challenge. Each year would end with Annie being able to look back on a year filled with projects and progress, more mission projects at work and more societies. Even as the frontier boxes began to go all over the west, missionary societies were beginning in those frontier churches. More women and children were involved in telling the good news. At the end of 1890, Annie stopped one evening to take stock of the year. She had written 2,737 letters. She began a list of new work and was amazed at how much God had accomplished through women who willingly worked together. That first year, seventy-one boxes had been sent to the missionary families, and the numbers grew each year.

A big centennial for 100 years of missionary service overseas was now in the planning. To no one's surprise, women were a very big part of it. Annie liked to think of all God had done since the first missionaries, Ann and Adoniram Judson, had sailed for Burma in 1812. Also, along with plans for a huge centennial celebration, Southern Baptists, in 1891, voted to establish their own Sunday School Board and begin publishing their own literature. Annie began to think up all sorts of ideas about how WMU could cooperate with the Sunday School Board in addition to the two mission boards. Another new outreach!

Alice Armstrong, with her usual sweet spirit and talented pen, began writing for the Sunday School Board, and her words reached into thousands of homes across America. Alice, just like her sister Annie, never took a salary for their many hours of work each week. Never a day passed that the sisters were not busy and involved. And there were very few days that passed without Miss Armstrong pondering in her creative mind what she needed to do next. Take the immigrant population. Annie had been thinking about them since she was a young girl exploring Baltimore with her brother James. People came by the thousands to Baltimore Harbor and then spread across the United States. Annie passed immigrants each day in the streets of her city and kept pondering on her childhood wish — to help all these little children who were strangers in a strange land. Who could have known that this very need would one day come knocking at Annie Armstrong's office door?

The Rest of the Story

Baltimore was an amazing fit for WMU work with immigrants. From the time Annie had been a primary school child growing up in the bustling harbor city, immigrant children had captured her heart. She had an uncanny ability to put herself in their place, and to think of what it would feel like if *she* was a little one in a strange, foreign place where nothing looked, sounded or tasted familiar. It must be dreadfully lonely. Sure enough, many years later the grown-up Annie fulfilled her childhood wish and helped those little ones feel welcome.

Gavel made from a stairway in Annie's home church. It was presented to WMU by Maryland WMU in 1963. The gold plate on the gavel reads: SBC-WMU-MD 1888-1963. (Courtesy of National Woman's Missionary Union)

Marie Buhlmaier, beloved longtime Southern Baptist missionary to immigrants in America. (Courtesy of Home Mission Board, SBC, 1924)

Chapter Seven

Annie and the New Arrivals
1890s

A brisk autumn breeze stirred the fallen leaves along the sidewalk as Annie and Alice Armstrong made their familiar walk to the WMU office.

"Alice," Annie smiled as she looked at her sister, "I'm so happy that fall is here and we are starting our new WMU year. Now we can get back to work!"

Alice gave a disbelieving chuckle, "Sister, you have worked all through our summer vacation, so what is *different?*"

Annie laughed as she agreed, "Oh, I mean I'm glad to be getting back to my desk and really getting organized and working on projects — old ones, new ones. I can't think of anything much more satisfying."

Office was like home. Annie smoothed out her long black skirt as she sat down in her familiar chair. Giving a sigh of satisfaction, she noted the stack of letters waiting for her eyes. *Now to see what challenges lie ahead this year,* Annie told herself.

Right on top of the stack was a letter from Fannie Heck. Annie's thoughts returned to last year when her friend Mattie McIntosh stepped down as president of WMU. Mattie explained that she could not serve a fifth year; however, she discussed with Annie a young woman whom she felt would make an excellent president. "Annie, I have had my eye on Miss Heck of North Carolina. She has so many helpful ideas. Also, the women love her and easily follow her lead."

Annie nodded in agreement, "Mattie, I think you have a good idea. I am quite impressed with Fannie Heck. She is both brilliant and far-thinking. And," Annie concluded, "Fannie has a 'presence' about her. Women look to her for guidance."

To Annie's delight, WMU unanimously elected Fannie as president. Now, as Annie arranged her tasks for the day, she reflected on her work with Fannie. She really did have some new and challenging ideas. Annie recalled the highlight of last year's meeting. Lottie Moon herself was there. The audience was especially attentive when tall and elegant Fannie Heck introduced the famous China missionary. There stood the four-foot-seven-inch lady who was their hero. The ladies all knew this moment in Lottie's presence was a never-to-be-forgotten occasion.

But right now, Annie was worried about Fannie Heck. Fannie's beloved father was seriously ill. Even more than usual, the Heck family now depended on Fannie. Additionally, Fannie was struck with a terrifying, painful disease of the eyes. She was unable to be up and doing. Annie hoped this just a temporary sickness. WMU needed Fannie's talent and leadership.

Now, hesitantly, Annie opened the letter. She was aware of the of the hum of voices from the nearby office rooms and the *click-click-click* of a typewriter. Annie smiled to herself, silently thanking God all over again for the invention of typewriters — what a time-saver they were. But, as she read Fannie's letter, Annie drew in a surprised breath. She called out, "Alice, could you come here a moment, please?" Recognizing the anxiety in Annie's voice, Alice hurried in from the next room. "Sister," Annie sounded worried, "please look at this letter from Miss Heck."

Alice began reading, quickly stopping and drawing in a surprised breath. "Oh no, Annie. Miss Heck is so ill she cannot be nominated for re-election as president."

Annie nodded, "Alice, I really regret this. We will just have to pray for healing and God's help."

Alice looked into her sister's concerned eyes and put a comforting hand on her shoulder, "Annie, we will go forward. You know that. God will lead us clearly."

Heaving a big sigh, Annie smoothed her crisp black skirt as she sat again and reached for the next letter waiting for her. Thinking out loud, Annie murmured, *Dear Lord, lead us in the right way.* Her first task was to separate the correspondence into stacks. The first pile was letters about new projects WMU was helping. Next to that came a pile that concerned the needs for frontier boxes. This work was so dear to Annie's heart, and women everywhere were enthusiastic and helping with boxes.

At that moment, one of the office volunteers stuck her head in the door, saying, "Miss Annie, we have a visitor from New York. Miss Marie Buhlmaier would like to see you."

Annie stood up immediately to greet the short and neatly dressed young woman entering the door. In a glance, she took in the smooth brown hair pulled back, the crisp white collar and the immaculate grey suit. Annie's eyes sparkled as she stepped forward and warmly grasped Marie's hand.

"Miss Buhlmaier, I am delighted to finally meet you. Thank you for coming from New York City."

"Miss Armstrong," Marie responded, and her soft grey eyes twinkled. "It is *my* honor to meet the lady who leads WMU. "I am so excited that it was your invitation that brings me to Baltimore to work. In fact," she continued, it is because of you that our Home Mission Board has appointed me as a missionary to immigrants coming to America!"

The two women, one so tall and elegant, the other short and trim, were a real contrast as they beamed at one another.

Annie remarked, "Marie, I love your crisp accent. Were you born in Germany?"

Marie smiled, "Yes, I was nine years old when I arrived in America. And," she nodded her head, "I so well remember what it felt like to be a stranger in a strange land. That is one reason I am so excited about this calling to work with immigrants. I, too, was brand new to America." Her face grew wistful as she added, "I wish someone had been on the wharf to welcome this scared little nine-year-old to a big, strange, new country."

Annie's eyes were full of sympathy, "Miss Buhlmaier, when I was a young girl about that same age, I followed my brother around Baltimore. Every day, we would see foreign children, most of them young, who had just arrived in America. I used to say to my brother, 'James, it must feel so scary to be in a strange new place and not even be able to understand what people are saying.'" Annie added, "Miss Buhlmaier, I have never forgotten the frightened look in those little children's eyes. And now,

God is giving me — all Baptists — a chance to help them. And, that is thanks to you!"

Marie beamed, "Miss Annie, as soon as I get settled in this work, I want you to come one day to the docks with me to meet some ships. You can greet people with me!"

Giving a little nod of her head, Annie explained to her new friend, "There is one problem I have *always* had. I am terrible with foreign languages. And," she added, "I'm afraid I can't speak a word of German!"

Marie chuckled and shook her head, "Never mind, Miss Annie, everyone all over the world can understand a smile — and yours is beautiful!"

Annie was intrigued with the idea of visiting arriving ships. The two made plans to go together one day soon to meet incoming ships.

Upon inquiring, Marie learned that over 100,000 Germans already lived right in Baltimore. She would be able to tell them the gospel story as well as greet and help new immigrants. "Just think, Miss Armstrong," she exclaimed, "most of these newcomers have no idea of God's love for them. And now I will have an opportunity to tell them!"

Annie Armstrong spoke as she grasped Marie's hand and held it, "Marie, I want you to know that I am your friend." (In the years that followed, Marie Buhlmaier found Miss Annie to be one of her best friends and co-workers.)

Marie got to work at once. She met steamships loaded with people coming to start a new life in a new country. They brought all their earthly goods with them, and most of them had pitifully little. Hundreds of people walked down the ramp from ship to wharf, looking timid and frightened. How wonderful to be greeted with a friendly smile and a firm handshake. Then they heard a cheerful young voice speak in their own language. Marie greeted them all, saying, "Welcome to America, and may God bless you in your new home." Along with the smile and greeting came practical help. Marie helped with their luggage and answered their anxious questions. She helped them send telegrams to relatives in America and often soothed and cared for their babies who were fretful and crying. Many were given a fresh loaf of bread, and milk was provided for their babies.

Marie was always practical, giving new families a map of the United States, and providing them the names of German pastors in the part of the country where they were going. Most important, Marie gave them a Bible. What a treasure this became for many immigrants — a Bible in their own language. Miss Buhlmaier also gave each one a little tract telling about God's plan of salvation.

A few months later, Annie was excited to be able to go to the wharf with Marie and meet an incoming ship loaded with human cargo. It was overwhelming. There in the midst of them was a small, neat young woman with a winning smile and a hand stretched out to help. Annie was overwhelmed, and astounded at all that one small woman could accomplish in a short time.

As they met one large ship full of new immigrants, Annie watched in wonder as hundreds of anxious-looking people walked down the gangplank. They were greeted with the friendly and welcoming smile of Miss Buhlmaier. Annie caught the eyes of a little girl who looked about four. She was clinging for dear life to her mama's hand. The child looked way up and met the eyes of a very tall and slender lady dressed in a black skirt — a lady who gave her a sweet smile. Annie bent down from her great height and got on eye level with the little girl. She smiled into the child's eyes and placed a freshly baked bun in her hand. The little one looked at the bread and then up at the tall stranger. Her little face broke into a smile. Annie squeezed her hand and smiled broadly. She had made a new friend.

Annie was truly thankful that WMU was able to assist with

literature and funds to help so many people who badly needed it. Not only that, WMU women in the Baltimore area pitched in and helped immigrants who needed assistance. They also assisted in meeting the needs of many strangers who stayed in Baltimore. Annie pitched in personally and helped start a sewing school among the Germans who lived in Baltimore. These ladies then helped the new immigrants to learn the same skills. Every time Annie could help with ministry in person, she smiled to herself and breathed a little prayer of thankfulness. She well recalled the young nine-year-old Annie who wanted to help those frightened young children in her city. Now, she actually could do that very thing.

Germans were not the only immigrants who needed Bibles in their own language; there were immigrants from many other lands, also. About this same time, Baptists began a Sunday School Board to meet the need for Bible learning. Of course, Annie Armstrong was one of the key leaders behind the idea and helped the brand-new Sunday School Board get started. WMU was one of its best cheerleaders and helpers. When the new board began printing Bible material in several languages, Miss Buhlmaier's work with immigrants grew. Marie became a familiar sight on the docks, wearing a butcher's apron with lots of pockets, all filled with tracts and maps for newcomers. Baptists had a treasure in Marie Buhlmaier. She was one small woman, doing the work of several people and enjoying each opportunity to share God's love.

Now, in the late 1890s, Annie Armstrong had more to do every day than the day had hours. She loved it that way. Annie was more than busy with a multitude of projects and ministries, plus all the work of heading up a growing organization involved in helping tell the world about God and His love. Every day Annie went over in her mind all that needed doing: immigrants, frontier work, orphans, mountain schools mothers' meetings, Indians, helping each state WMU. Where would the time come from?

Life was rewarding but not easy for any in the Armstrong household in 1898. In fact, it had not been easy for quite a while. Annie and Alice's beloved mother was growing more frail every day.

Mary kept telling her daughters, "I am alright. You just do what you need to do." Annie and Alice exchanged a glance, "Mama, we will, but you need us too."

Annie looked searchingly into Alice's face. She read signs of exhaustion there. Alice was not well either. She spoke with force, "Sister, I think you need to rest. The doctors have been telling you that for months now. You can write here at home, and we do need your pen. But, you can also get some rest." Alice protested but knew at the same time that her sister was right. She was absolutely exhausted as well.

Annie considered for a moment and then continued. "I have been thinking for some time that I, too, need more time at home. Beginning tomorrow, I am going to work from home most of the time."

The next morning, Annie introduced the idea to Mary Armstrong. "Oh no," her mother protested, "how can you do that?"

Annie smiled comfortingly, "You'll see. I will bring my typewriter home, and I will have my main stenographer come here each day. She can help with all the letters!"

Alice shook her head in exasperation, "I should have known, Sister. That is what you have done for the past eleven years. You take your work *with* you! You literally have not had a vacation in all that time."

The leaves were turning all sorts of colors the autumn of 1898. Annie had been WMU's leader since it organized in 1888. This was her eleventh year, and she and Alice were keenly aware that their mother would not be with them much longer. Throughout the following month, Annie tirelessly worked from home each day, sending letters and messages back and forth to the office by her loyal helpers. On November 15, Mary

Armstrong went to be with the Lord whom she had faithfully served so many years. The daughters were stricken with grief but gave thanks that they were at her side. Annie wrote Dr. Willingham at the Foreign Mission Board, "We laid Mother away today, but I find it is easier for me to keep on working than to stop and to think of how we will miss her."

Being busy was a way to help Annie and Alice heal, and busy they were. Now was the time for Annie to travel. Annie was honest with herself. She liked routine. She liked having everything organized and working just right. Travel was like a chore to her. However, she needed to visit several states and assist their leadership. Furthermore, work was just getting ready to start with African American Baptist women in the country. (In Annie's day, people used the term "colored" people.) They had already called on Annie's help and she was eager to give it. Of course, giving help would take time.

But — a little bit of the child that was in Annie was still eager to see what might be around the corner and what might be her next adventure. She remembered her beloved brother James and their young dreams of adventure. Well, she had lost James to disease fifteen years earlier, but she imagined he would enjoy the adventures that were shaping up right ahead of her now.

The Rest of the Story

Marie Buhlmaier was a little-known Baptist heroine. She devoted her life to serving immigrants to America. When Marie was nine, her mother and younger siblings came to the New World to join her father. Marie was her mother's main help, and it was a scary time for a young child who had never been away from home. Her most cherished possession was her beautiful hand-crafted doll house full of lovely furnishings, made by her grandfather. It was dismantled and packed to travel to the New World. At the last minute, it had to be left behind.

There was no space. At night, Marie wept many tears over her precious treasure, a beloved piece of home. She never forgot that beautiful little house, but she determined to invest her life in helping hundreds of people find a new home in a new land. She welcomed thousands to America and helped many years with German immigrants in both Baltimore and Washington, D.C. Many a little baby born in the new land was given the name "Marie" for the kind little lady who had welcomed her and her family to a home in America.

Immigrants arriving at Locust Point pier, Baltimore, in the 1800s. (Courtesy of National Woman's Missionary Union)

Annie Armstrong's mounting rock at Tuskegee Church in Oklahoma Territory. At this church in 1900, Annie helped organize the first Woman's Missionary Society. Artist's rendering of Annie on a horse in front of the mounting rock. (Courtesy of Augusta Smith)

Chapter Eight

Go West, Miss Annie!
1896–1901

One dull, overcast November morning in 1896, Annie sat at her desk thinking about the amazing number of projects and needs that had crossed her desk in ten years. Some days she thought Baptist women had accomplished so much. Other times, she felt like WMU hadn't even made a good start. Just as Annie started the day's work, one of the volunteers tapped on the door. "Miss Annie, a Rev. Jordan from Washington to see you." Annie wracked her brain, *Do I know a Rev. Jordan?* She couldn't recall the name.

Rising to greet her guest, Annie shook hands with a tall, distinguished, middle-aged African American gentleman who immediately thanked her for giving him time on her schedule. Dr. Jordan got right to business, "Miss Armstrong, I am impressed with your ability to get things done, and to work with more than one group and bring them together." Annie gave him her full attention as he continued, "I am secretary of the Foreign Mission Board of National Baptists. And," he told her, "I am eager to see the Baptist women of *our* convention organize for missions. Who better than the founder of the Woman's Missionary Union to help us get started in the right way?" He concluded, "I have seen your success and how God is blessing missions efforts with Southern Baptists. We want to contribute our part."

Annie was intrigued. She had been involved in Baltimore work with colored women (the name for African American citizens in that century) for more than twenty years. This looked like the perfect opportunity to truly help them reach out to missions around the world. This might open exciting new doors to sharing the gospel in Africa! Dr. Jordan explained that his convention had recently identified a young woman who appeared likely to lead National Baptist women with real skill.

"Her name is Nannie Helen Burroughs," Rev. Jordan continued. "You will not believe her leadership potential and skills when I tell you she is not yet 18 years old. I believe God has endowed her with special talents and a unique spirit."

For a long moment, Annie sat still, her head tilted to one side, just looking at her guest and pondering his request. Never one to dally, Annie quickly made up her mind. "Dr. Jordan," she briskly said, "I am willing to trust your wisdom. I will approach our executive committee and arrange a meeting."

Rev. Jordan's faith in her ability touched Annie. Two months later, she and other WMU leaders met with Dr. Jordan and Miss Burroughs. Annie was immediately impressed with the tall young woman who shook her hand so firmly. Still not even 18 and not much shorter than Annie herself, Nannie Helen looked and acted older than her tender years. Her remarkable intelligence was noticeable. The meeting that lasted four hours was the beginning of a strong and passionate missions organization for National Baptist women. It was also the beginning of a life-long friendship between two outstanding leaders, Annie and Nannie. Annie thanked God for placing this opportunity in her lap.

Nannie asked Annie to speak at the first annual meeting of National Baptist Convention WMU. She was received as a celebrity. Scores of women wanted to personally thank her for helping them organize. Annie's message was the highlight of the meeting. "You are our treasured friend," she heard time and again from the women. Annie knew that the hand of God made this special relationship possible. (She could not know back then that Nannie Helen would go on to be one of America's leaders of women of that century. She even founded a school for girls in Washington, D.C.)

However, Miss Burroughs and her outreach was only one of the areas where Annie was hard at work. With one project after another, she wished she could put her whole time into that particular need. What to do? There were scores of worthy needs, and all demanding her attention. Annie discovered she needed to travel and work more effectively. Travel tired her, but it was necessary. Travel took time, but it needed doing.

One evening, as Annie prepared for yet another trip, Alice took one look at her sister's face and shook her head, "Annie, you are driving yourself to an early grave." She sighed and added, "I know only too well all you do. And, I know how many records you manage to keep."

Alice was curious, "Sister, just how many letters have you written in a single year?"

Annie gave a rueful laugh, "Two years ago — I think the total count for that year was 17,700 letters."

Annie unconsciously rubbed her writing hand as she thought of all those letters. (Her hands would hurt the rest of her life because of those thousands of letters each year.)

Giving a chuckle, Alice shook her head in disbelief, "Annie, it makes *my* hand hurt just to *think* about writing so many!"

One morning as Alice sat at her desk writing for one of the articles she regularly prepared for journals, she heard Annie calling, "Alice, can you come look at this?"

Quickly, Alice entered her sister's office, "Annie, is there a problem?" One look at Annie's face told her must be a happy problem.

Annie was grinning. "Sister," she beamed, "just read this letter."

Alice glanced at the signature. *Dr. Willingham.* This was from the Foreign Mission Board. As she scanned the letter, Alice began smiling too, "Oh, Sister, what a great letter!"

The Foreign Mission Board had been heading up the Sunbeam Band (now called Mission Friends) ever since "Uncle George" Braxton Taylor, the founder of Sunbeams, had turned it over to them.

Annie was thrilled. "Just think, Alice, the board now wants WMU to lead the Sunbeams. The dearest dream of my heart — training the children in missions! And I know Miss Heck will be thrilled too," she concluded. "She thinks training the children is the most important step to the future of missions!" (In those early days the Sunbeam Band included children from 4 to 14. So, Annie's "little people" were both little and not so little. All ages were dear to her heart.)

Women in each state began leading Sunbeam groups, and the numbers grew rapidly. As WMU grew, so did Annie's responsibilities. She encouraged all the state leaders and worked closely with whoever was elected each year as national WMU president. Some presidents were quiet, and others more outspoken. Sister Alice noticed her sister was more at ease with the presidents who agreed with Annie's ideas and let her take the lead. This was a distinct part of Annie's personality. However, the presidents did not always wholeheartedly agree with Annie.

Most noticeable among the early presidents was Fannie Heck. She was re-elected unanimously by all the states when she recovered from her illness in 1895. Fannie was brilliant and farsighted in her thinking. In both these ways, she was much like Annie herself. Sister Alice watched from the sidelines the relationship of each president with her sister. She could see that Miss Heck was not content to be just a smiling face and preside gracefully at annual meetings. Fannie felt the women had elected her to work and help. That is what a president should do. Annie certainly recognized Fannie's many talents, but she personally felt the job of a president was to support Annie herself.

Alice knew her sister so well. One day, when Annie was questioning a decision of Fannie's with which she herself did not agree, Alice looked keenly into her eyes and remarked, "Sister, do you realize how much you and Miss Heck are alike?"

Annie was shocked. Her eyebrows rose as she retorted, "Oh no! She and I have the exact opposite view."

Alice nodded, "Ah, yes, Annie, but just like you, Fannie is *certain* that she is right. She feels it is her job to represent the views of the ladies who elected her." Annie did not respond to that observation; she knew in her heart that her sister was right.

In the ten years that WMU had been an organization, Annie Armstrong was not only the leader but also the main person to make decisions and plan the future. The executive committee in Baltimore knew and loved her. They would quickly agree with her ideas, sometimes not recognizing that listening to more than one view could be a healthy thing. Fannie Heck, on the other hand, believed that several different viewpoints should be considered and decisions be made by the whole group. Things grew quite tense; often, Annie and Fannie often did not agree on how to handle an issue. Annie was sure *her* view was the right one. On the other hand, Fannie was just as certain *her* conclusion was the right one. How could they resolve this situation?Meanwhile, the men who headed the mission boards recognized this problem. They needed WMU to be effective and to work cooperatively with the other boards. The men understood that if the women were not working with each *other*, it would affect *all* the boards. So, the leaders of the foreign mission, home mission, and Sunday School boards met with Annie and Fannie to discuss this issue. In the end, Annie came out and bluntly said, "I am sorry. If Miss Heck remains as president, I must resign." The board leaders were shocked. They knew how Miss Armstrong always spoke her mind. They also realized she had a quick temper, although she could just as quickly get over it. On the other hand, Miss Heck was also a brilliant and visionary woman. She just did not speak her mind quickly like Annie did.

In that meeting, tension in the room could be cut with a knife. Fannie Heck thought long and steadily. At long last, she took a deep breath and softly but firmly spoke up, "That must not happen. Baptist women look to Miss Armstrong for leadership. They always have." Fannie quietly but firmly concluded, "I will withdraw my name as a candidate for re-election at our coming meeting." Fannie did just that. She resigned at the annual meeting in May. (Less than ten years later, Annie resigned as corresponding secretary. At that 1906 annual meeting, Fannie Heck was unanimously re-elected president. She served until her death in 1915.)

Alice knew better than anyone how hard Annie was driving herself. She worked from early morning until late at night. She never went home from the office without work in her satchel. Alice was aware that her beloved sister had not taken a vacation in more than ten years. But, even she didn't know that Annie's doctors told her she was ruining her health; they prescribed several months of rest. Annie did not follow that prescription. She came to understand years later that she should have listened to her doctors. However, some who worked with Annie recognized what she was doing to herself. Dr. Willingham of the Foreign Mission Board was deeply concerned. He wrote Alice, warning, "What is going to happen to your work if you break down and are laid aside from overwork — or after we have had a great funeral and tell of how much good you have done, and *could* have done, if you had lived longer. I am thinking every now and then, that we can glorify God by resting some."

But to Annie's mind, there was work to do. Work meant travel, and Annie began to plan trips. There was a crying need for more churches to organize women's societies. The personal touch was needed. This meant traveling. Travel would take time; there were no airplanes in 1900. The fastest travel was by train (the Iron Horse): dirty, tedious, tiring trains. Annie needed to visit the states one by one. And, no one had approached the West to start building mission societies there. Ever since their first project to help the indigenous people in Indian Territory thirty years earlier, Annie had a dream in her heart. She wanted to go West. She wanted to personally help the people there.

That meant travel. A plan took shape in her fertile mind. The states between Maryland and the West needed personal encouragement to start new societies. Then why not help them, and then go further on west? Just thinking about the length of such a trip and the amount of time involved was daunting, even to a tireless person like Annie. The August morning she was to leave Baltimore, Annie looked at the itinerary and gave a little gulp. Forty days? Four thousand miles? But then the excitement of fulfilling a dream of many years smothered her doubts and fears. She had prayed it through — and, furthermore, she had a travel companion. (In that day, women did not travel alone, and

Annie had a new friend who was going with her.)

She recalled the day Anna Schimp first walked into her office. Quiet, reserved, Mrs. Schimp came to see Miss Armstrong because she wanted to give money away! Anna Schimp was from Switzerland. She and her husband, a wealthy businessman, had immigrated to America years earlier. Sadly, he died, and Mrs. Schimp, a woman of deep faith, wanted to use their money to bless other people and bring people to faith in Christ. She began by joining WMU. Annie was intrigued to hear Mrs. Schimp's first idea. She wanted to give $4,000 to Southern Baptists to begin an annuity fund that would help faithful pastors have a retirement in their old age. This rang a loud bell with Annie. For years, Annie had felt like Baptists really needed such a program. She happily agreed to help Anna Schimp get such an annuity program started.

Mrs. Schimp spoke firmly, "Miss Armstrong, there is one condition. I don't want anyone to know I am giving the money." Annie gladly agreed. That very day Annie found a new friend, a woman who shared her spiritual vision.

In turn, Anna was thrilled to accompany Annie on a trip west. Her eyes sparkled at such a chance. At once, she agreed to take charge of the travel arrangements and relieve Miss Armstrong of that responsibility. Therefore, it was two excited women who set out together in August on a brand-new adventure in a brand-new century.

At last! Annie had been waiting for such an experience ever since she began sewing uniforms for indigenous students in Indian Territory nearly twenty years earlier. She was going West! Thoughts of her brother James flitted across Annie's mind. *Wouldn't James love such a trip.* She glanced at quiet, little Anna Schimp, her travel companion. Anna was a calm and steady woman, but even she was sparkling with enthusiasm at this amazing adventure. They were going to visit many states, and then — Indian Territory! (In that century, indigenous people were called Indians.) Anna discovered that her new friend Annie was a record keeper. She carefully recorded each mile traveled, each speech made, each state, each town, and every home visited. Annie met with WMU groups in those states and inspired women all along the way. The scenery out their train window changed from beautiful green trees and rolling hills to fewer trees and more open plains. The weather grew hotter and drier as well. Towns grew more scattered along the way.

And finally, Oklahoma! Annie was fascinated by what she had learned about the indigenous population of America. These were people who had been in this land before any Europeans had ever heard of such a place. Annie was also surprised to learn that in the early days of the century, Creek and Seminole tribes had organized women's societies — even before WMU had organized back in 1888.

The heat! Annie and Anna had heard about it. Neither, however, had experienced heat like this. Everywhere, they saw dust clouds. Often as they traveled in an open buggy, or in a cart, and certainly on horseback, the dust could be so thick it was choking. Nonetheless, dust did not choke their enthusiasm. They were in the West and were meeting brave frontiersmen and indigenous people of many tribes. All these people had the same heart needs.

Anna observed Annie each day as she recorded their journey in a little notebook. Time on the train gave Annie a chance to catch up on records. During this first trip West (the first of five), Annie's heart was full of what she saw and experienced. In forty days, she attended fifty-nine meetings and made thirty-nine speeches. The many people who had heard of the amazing Miss Armstrong now met her in person, a tall and commanding figure whose smile came right from her heart. From weather-worn frontier women in calico dresses to tribal women in their garments of cowhide, none ever forgot this remarkable lady who quickly became their friend. She won the hearts of the frontier missionary pastors as well. She called them her "substitutes," for they were the ones on the field doing the work.

When Annie entered the teepees on the reservations to greet women, she had to stoop to enter through the cowhide flaps that served as entrances. The women of the various tribes, from Osage to Choctaw to Pawnee, would give her three firm shakes of the hand. This traditional greeting of welcome warmed Annie's heart each time. These women had so little yet wanted to organize societies and to give money so others could learn of God's love too.

Annie would never forget her visits in the homes of frontier missionaries as well. Most of them were educated men and women who had left the comforts of home behind to bring the gospel to the frontier. One of Annie's first visits was in the home of a missionary couple in Blackwell, Oklahoma. A grandmother and grandfather lived with them, along with four children. Annie noted that the family had just four small rooms — two beds, four chairs, and a rocking chair. The missionary's salary was $200 a year, and $100 of that went for rent. All their clothing came from WMU frontier boxes. Annie looked around in amazement and vowed to do even more about promoting those boxes.

Of course, Annie was drawn to the children. How she loved "little people," as she lovingly named them. The youngest, four years old, was in awe of the tall, slender lady with the beautiful, braided hair piled high on her head. She looked like she had stepped out of a story book. Annie knelt on eye level with the little sprite and placed a stick of hard candy into her small hands. The child's eyes grew big, and she drew in her breath — a piece of candy, and it wasn't even Christmas! That little girl never forgot the moment.

Forty days later, Annie and Anna were back on the Iron Horse headed back to Baltimore. Both of them felt dusty and both had lost weight. Nonetheless, Annie's eyes were glowing.

She leaned back on the train seat, gave a happy sigh and turned to Anna. "My friend," she smiled, "are you completely worn out?"

Anna smiled in return as she replied, "Wellllll, maybe a trifle," and her eyes twinkled.

Annie reached over to pat her friend's knee, remarking, "I hope you aren't too weary to do it all again! I'm already planning a trip back to the reservations. But I promise to wait a little while!" she added comfortingly.

Forty days and 4,000 miles later, a completely exhausted but happily satisfied Annie Armstrong returned home. Her eyes and mind and heart were brim full of all she had seen and experienced. She made herself a silent promise that she would return to the frontier again. (She kept that promise to herself, again, and again, and yet again.)

The Rest of the Story

For all the years Annie Armstrong remained as WMU's first leader, she constantly supported and encouraged Nannie Helen Burroughs, who led National Baptist Convention women. No matter how much was going on, Annie always had time to assist Nannie. She was a truly remarkable young woman. Jennie Burroughs, her mother, was born enslaved. Her baby Nannie was born free in 1879. However, there were very few opportunities for education for African Americans. Nannie Helen was motivated by one little word: She was determined to change *no* into *yes*.

Annie Armstrong became her role model for a Christian leader. Nannie Helen was a wonderful orator and often electrified audiences with her persuasive and inspiring speeches. Nannie served as the director of National Baptist Convention women until her death at the age of 82. Miss Annie encouraged Nannie, opened doors for her, and led the way in leadership. Nannie went on to found a school for African American girls in Washington, D.C. The school's motto: "We specialize in the impossible."

Nannie said of Miss Annie, "To me, Miss Armstrong was a symbol of what a woman could do. She fired my soul." In later years, this great African American leader stated: "If I could, I would erect the finest monument I could, in honor of Miss Armstrong, who did so much to help and encourage Negro Baptist Women." (It was, indeed, Annie Armstrong who was the forerunner among Southern Baptists in interracial relations. This was just one of the many achievements she left as a legacy.)

The remarkable Nannie Helen Burroughs (1879-1961), who, at age 22, became the first leader of National Baptist Women, and was mentored by Annie Armstrong. (Courtesy of National Woman's Missionary Union)

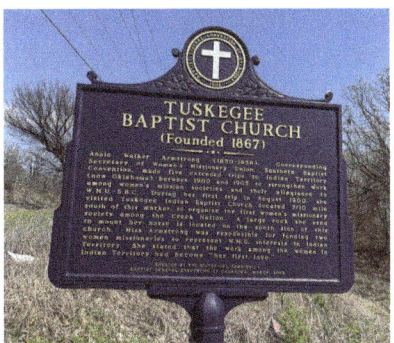

Historical marker, Tuskegee Baptist Church, Oklahoma, founded 1867. (Courtesy of Augusta Smith)

Chapter Nine

TRAVELS NEAR AND FAR
1901–1902

The Armstrong sisters walked home that July evening following the special appointment service at Eutaw Place Church. Their cousin Mary Grace Levering Evans and her doctor husband, Phillip, were headed to China as missionaries.

"Sister, how we are going to miss Mary Grace when she leaves," Annie sighed as she and Alice neared their house. "But isn't it wonderful to know she is our 'substitute,' telling the good news in China?"

Alice smiled broadly as she responded, "Annie, it does my heart good to think of all she and Phillip will be doing. Just imagine all the travel ahead of them."

Annie added to the thought, "And we will want to pray for them just like we would want people to pray for *us* if we were the ones going."

Annie changed the subject a moment later as she sighed and admitted, "Alice, I know you will fuss at me, but I need to travel again."

It was Alice's turn to sigh as she pleaded, "Sister, you *must* try to slow down and not overdo. Where are you headed now?"

Annie explained, "Actually, I'm not going *far* away, but I need to spend time encouraging women in our nearby states, like Kentucky and Tennessee."

Annie spent August and September on a marathon tour, traveling more than 2,000 miles in four states, meeting and encouraging women. She spent time in Nashville with Nannie Helen Burroughs and spoke at a large gathering of National Baptist women. All the while, she marveled at what an incredible leader young Nannie was becoming. And to think, she wasn't even 25 yet! A few weeks later, Annie shook her head as she read over her notes about the trip she had just finished. *No wonder I feel exhausted,* she thought. In those fifty days she had spoken in thirty places.

Not a month later, Alice was dismayed to learn her intrepid sister was headed out again. However, she was relieved that this trip was just to the eastern shore in Maryland. Alice's relief didn't last long when Annie got home and told of her adventures on that winter trip.

"Alice," Annie reported, "the heat of Indian Territory was *nothing* compared to the bitter cold of this Maryland trip! I met with six churches in four days." She grimaced as she recalled, "One freezing night, I had to stay in a bedroom with four broken window panes. And, picture this, Sister. I literally watched ice form around me." Annie finished her account of the Maryland trip, concluding, "Now I get to come home to our warm house. But I stand in awe of all those faithful women who keep the church alive in difficult conditions right here in our state."

Between Annie's numerous trips, she was daily at her office. She realized that her "happy place" was at her desk, answering letters and

Travels Near and Far: 1901–1902

responding to needs both near and far. And, year after year, her sister observed Annie's special talent. No matter what the different personalities were like, Annie had the knack for being able to bring agreement of opinion among the leaders of the different boards. The men frequently did not agree with each other — but somehow Miss Armstrong was able to get them to work together for the good of all. Annie had the gift of bringing mutual agreement out of very different opinions. She was also continually creative, coming up with original ideas for how to do things. Yet always, Annie managed to give the credit for those ideas to the people with whom she worked. It was a rare gift. Her satisfaction came from an idea coming to life. She didn't relish credit for planning it all. Annie's special joy was seeing people work together.

One piece of furniture in Annie's office, a couch, gave her particular delight. The couch gladdened Sister Alice's heart as well, for occasionally Annie would actually take a quick rest in the middle of her busy day. This couch was on loan from the Foreign Mission Board and was the reclining sofa on which her hero, Ann Judson, had lain a century earlier as she recovered from a deadly liver disease. Just lying on that couch gave Annie a special feeling of being part of Baptists' missions spirit. Ann Judson's motto had been "Bless God and Take Courage." Annie felt like she also needed to do the same, especially when work got tough.

Annie's usual spot, though, was either working at her desk, attending a meeting and speaking, or traveling to yet another needy place. She admitted to one of the board leaders that she would be perfectly content not to have to endlessly attend meetings — they wore her out. Nonetheless, when Annie was needed at a gathering, or a meeting, she was there, helping and encouraging women and young people.

However, right up there with her joy and pleasure in office work was her love for time on the frontier and in Indian Territory. Annie was convinced that the center for mission leadership would be in the West by the middle of the century. (And she was right in her prediction. Her trips to the frontier helped pave the way.)

Summer arrived in 1902, and Annie and Anna Schimp were on their way west again — this time, headed to Oklahoma Territory and then on to Mexico. Annie was very hesitant about going to a foreign country. It was that old fear of hers about not being able to speak a foreign language. She decided, however, that she would just *swallow* her fear and see the needs of a whole new culture.

First though, she was excited about getting back to the frontier, seeing her frontier missionary friends, and visiting in the small frontier churches. Best of all, she was going to various reservations and visiting friends. She would make new ones as well. Sister Alice was worried about her, because this really *was* going to be a long trip — over 8,000 miles and eighty days. Annie commented to her faithful companion, Anna Schimp, that it might be best not to think of all 8,000 miles but just take it a day at a time. Annie equipped herself with a good supply of her handy notebooks so she could record their adventures along the way. As she studied about the frontier, she was astounded to learn that the frontier field was an area as large as France, Germany, and Great Britain combined.

Frontier missionaries greeted their tall and regal visitor from Baltimore like a part of the family who had come home. Annie, with her wonderful letter-writing skill, had developed the habit of writing her frontier missionary friends long, newsy letters. They knew she loved them and prayed for them each day. Annie was thrilled to see how the frontier work had grown in a short time. She had been right. The frontier people had very little, but on her first visit, Annie had encouraged them to sacrifice and give something themselves, to help the rest of the world know about God. These special women remembered her challenge, and that is what they did; now they felt the joy of being a part of sharing

Travels Near and Far: 1901–1902

God's love everywhere.

Sometimes Annie and Anna spent the night in a frontier home that was dug out in the side of a hill. Sometimes they slept on the floor of the small local church. Annie grinned when she recalled the night she had slept on a mattress with only one sheet. Thankfully, that was in the heat of summer.

As always, Annie's special joy was time on the reservations. The Christian women of the different tribes greeted her like a long-awaited friend. One of the churches even had a special "mounting rock" for Miss Annie, to help her mount her horse as she visited yet another reservation. Annie loved to share the tribal handshake, three firm shakes of the hand, with each lady. When they met in a large teepee, Annie and Anna, like their indigenous friends, sat cross-legged on the hard packed ground. It must have been terribly difficult when wearing a long skirt, but Annie never missed a beat. She fit right in with the other ladies, and they loved her for it. Several times, Annie would get a faraway look in her eyes and say to Anna, "Oh, if only I had five years to live here and organize the work. That would be such joy."

One hot, late-summer afternoon, Annie and Anna were headed to yet another reservation. In the distance, they saw the dust of a lone rider on his horse, coming quickly in their direction. For some reason, Annie felt no fear of meeting a stranger out on the lone prairie. The rider drew near, a man who looked slightly older than Annie. Seated on horseback, he lifted his hat and politely bowed, asking, "Are you Miss Annie Armstrong?" Annie had never seen the man, but kindly greeted him with, "Yes, I am Annie." He responded by introducing himself as a frontier missionary.

With a broad smile, he told her, "I have a story to tell you. Back in 1865, near the end of the Civil War, I was a young Union soldier in a prison camp in Baltimore. We were visited by kind women who helped us. I will never forget one of them, a Mrs. Mary Armstrong. She gave Bibles to several of us. They were treasures," he continued. "In the flyleaf of my Bible was written *Annie W. Armstrong*. Mrs. Armstrong told me this Bible was a gift from her daughter. It was this precious book that led to my conversion. Now, I am a frontier missionary. I recently learned that the leader of Woman's Missionary Union was coming to Oklahoma, and that her name was Annie W. Armstrong of Baltimore." By this time, the rider was beaming, and Annie was close to tears. He concluded, "I have ridden thirty miles, Miss Armstrong, to thank you for how you have blessed my life." That night, a tearful Annie recorded in her faithful journal the "sweet surprise" of the day that the Lord had sent her way.

This trip to Oklahoma was special to Annie in multiple ways. On her first trip to the territory, Annie had spoken to children's groups in small frontier churches. She emphasized to each child how important it was that *they* give too. They were not too young to make a difference. Annie suggested, "When you make contributions, divide the money into thirds. Use one portion for local needs, one for home missions, and one for foreign missions." When Annie returned to her office, she sent the children little "mite barrels" in which to save the money. Now, two years later, the children in one small church were so excited. *Miss Annie was coming again!* They proudly handed her two little barrels. The Sunbeams in Indian Territory had raised $14.52 so children in home and foreign lands could know Jesus too. No gift touched Annie's heart more than did those little sacrificial barrels, given from the hearts of children who themselves had so little.

Likewise, on her first trip to Oklahoma, Annie had helped several very small churches organize. She emphasized to the women who had so little that they, too, could be part of taking the gospel to the world. Any sacrifice was precious in God's sight. On this trip, Annie was seeing the truth of that statement played out. One shabbily dressed woman in a little frontier town had listened and responded for herself and the others. She gave sacrificially, and happily said to their visitor, "Sister Annie, now we no longer belong only to this little town, but we feel that we are part of God's great universe."

Annie and Anna never complained about the lack of comforts and conveniences on their weeks in Oklahoma Territory. They saw so clearly all the sacrifices the frontier missionaries around them made every day. Even sleeping on the floor in a little church building was alright. Annie sometimes smiled to herself and thought, *I am really going to enjoy my good bed when we get home to Baltimore!* Annie's heart always beat faster when she had time on the reservations with her friends in the various tribes. In teepee after teepee, Annie would sit, tribal fashion, and tell eager women about "the Jesus way." She listened joyfully as woman after woman told about how they were now walking "the Jesus way." Annie was thrilled to hear how Chief Lone Wolf, a Kiowa chief, was no longer scalping men. He was a deacon now in a Baptist church, and his wife was president of the missionary society!

On the Osage reservation, Annie was excited to learn that some Christians from the Kiowa tribe had come to Pawhuska, on the Osage reservation, to share the good news of the Jesus road. At the meeting that night, Annie drank in all that took place in the service, storing up memories to take home with her. She noticed one blanketed Osage standing apart from the other braves who were seated on the ground. Annie quietly stepped to his side and asked, "Can you understand about the Jesus way?" He looked at her earnestly and replied, "I can, if you will tell it to me." Annie told him the story of Jesus, and then the two of them knelt to pray. That evening, the Osage brave asked Christ into his heart. It was a moment forever printed on Annie's heart.

Annie left Oklahoma with a pang to her heart. How she loved time with such amazing friends. Once more, she told the many friends in the tribes and friends in the small frontier churches, "I am praying for you, and I will be back." (She made three more trips.)

Lying just ahead of her was another journey. Annie had lived over half a century, but this would be the first time she would go to a foreign country. Although, earlier in the year, Cousin Joshua Levering invited Annie to travel to China with them to see their daughter Mary and her doctor husband, Phillip, brand new missionaries in Yangchow. Annie would love such an adventure; however, the trip would last six months, and they would visit several countries — a glorious excursion. Annie felt like crying when she turned down the trip. She could not be away from her work that long. But now, here she was, at work and visiting Mexico, a foreign land.

As they boarded the train for Mexico, Annie confessed to her traveling companion, "Anna, I've always been hopeless with foreign languages. I wonder how I can help these people here when I can't speak their language?" She sounded anxious. Anna Schimp reached over and patted her knee, "Annie, I can't imagine you *anywhere* where you are not helping others. Just wait," she finished, "God has gone before us. He will bless our time here."

The weeks in Mexico were a revelation to Annie. She saw people in a land so near her own, but so different in culture and customs. She learned something new each day. Annie had been anticipating adventures along the way, and she had them. Some of them were not exactly the kind of adventure she expected. That included their train trip across the border. On the journey, men tried to wreck the train. Annie wrote to her sister Alice about the scary moments, saying, "My big self was in great danger." Their engine plunged over a steep embankment and the baggage car wrecked. "But," Annie wrote, "by a miracle the passengers were saved." After she got back to Baltimore, Annie further jolted Alice by telling of another train trip in Mexico. She and Anna Schimp had to wait four extra hours for their late train. The stationmaster explained that the train had been held up by robbers and one person killed. Alice was simply thankful she didn't learn about this while Annie was on the trip. It was frightening enough to hear about it later.

Mexico was beautiful in places, with lush green fields and beautiful flowers. It was heartbreaking in others. Annie saw more deep poverty than she could have imagined. On one hand, there were beautiful churches, a splendid palace, magnificent cathedrals. On the other, Annie was horrified at the poverty of so many of Mexico's people. She grieved at the sight of so many children who didn't know what it was like to not be hungry.

More than once, Annie commented to Anna, "I grew up in Baltimore and thought I *knew* Catholicism, but I had no idea how Roman Catholicism could control the lives of people." In Mexico, she saw how the priests controlled the people by their brand of religion. The custom was to baptize babies — but parents had to pay $2.25 to do that. This was impossible for a couple who had no money at all. To get married, a couple had to pay the priest anywhere between $15 and $40. People simply could not afford to marry in the church. No wonder the church buildings were so magnificent, and the people so poor. Annie's heart was broken. More than ever, she earnestly prayed for the missionaries who daily worked to help the people understand that salvation is *free*. It was God's gift.

The missionaries were wonderful to Annie and her companion. She finally relaxed and realized she could minister in a strange land even if she couldn't speak the language. The kind missionaries translated for her, and frequently in churches she spoke to the "little people." She dearly loved to teach children. One afternoon in one of the mission chapels, a little Mexican boy climbed up into Annie's lap. Looking way up into the tall lady's sparkling brown eyes, the little fellow was wide-eyed. Then he hesitantly touched her smooth white hand and asked, "Mi amigo?" (my friend?). Annie beamed into the earnest little eyes and responded, "Si." He then spoke just four words and they touched her tender heart, "Then do not go." That moment was forever imprinted in her heart. It sparkled like a jewel in the midst of an ordinary day. Annie could not know how her beautiful smile "spoke" the language of love to that little boy and every child she met along her journey.

The two ladies from Baltimore fell in love with the missionaries in Mexico. The Chevins, Mr. and Mrs. Watkins, the Mars, and the other missionaries were giving themselves wholeheartedly to the people they served. Annie, who prayed for so many missionaries in countless places, vowed to pray even harder. Her "substitutes" in the different countries were her heroes. Annie left Mexico with a new vision in her heart. In typical Annie style, she wanted to do something for the precious children she had come to love. She immediately sent back treats for "Christmas festivals" for the little ones in church after church scattered across Mexico. Forever in her heart was a new vision of the needs of the world. People everywhere needed to know how much God loved them.

Annie arrived home, and into the arms of her dear sister, completely exhausted. But she was also elated at the privilege of seeing another world. To be able to help somebody else each day along the way was a privilege she did not take lightly. And now, with a good night's sleep, she would happily face the pile of mail that was waiting for her the next morning in her office. After all, her desk was her happy place, the place where work was joy. It was just as well Annie could not know what troubled waters lay right ahead of her.

The Rest of the Story

In the midst of Annie Armstrong's massive workload, the opportunities she had with children never failed to give her the most joy. She had to travel so much that in the last few years, Annie had to give up her beloved "infants class," her Sunday school children. *Today is Christmas Eve,* Annie recalled with surprise. She had gotten so busy she nearly forgot. Stopping a moment, she thought nostalgically about Christmases gone by. Thinking about the joy of Christmas with little ones, and seeing their wonder and joy, made her heart wistful. Annie remembered the fun parties she used to give for the orphan children at the Home of the Friendless. She missed those days.

Just at that moment, one of the clerks came to the office door to tell Miss Armstrong a young man wanted to see her. She was surprised to learn a stranger was coming to the office at this late hour on December 24. When she shook hands with the tall young visitor, he spoke, "Miss Armstrong, you can't remember me, but years ago, I was one of your little boys at the Home of the Friendless." Annie smiled a welcome as she invited him in.

He handed her an envelope, explaining, "Miss Annie, I do not know of anyone that knows better how to make persons happy at Christmas than you do. Please use this money to help someone have a merry Christmas." That simple act of kindness rekindled the joy of Christmas in Annie's heart. She gratefully used that young man's gift to help give a Christmas dinner for poor people at her church.

Native praise choir, made up of indigenous women from many tribes in Oklahoma.. (Courtesy of Augusta Smith)

Sample cover of one of Annie Armstrong's many missions leaflets. (Courtesy of National Woman's Missionary Union)

Chapter Ten

Topsy Turvy Times
1903–1906

The more Annie traveled, the more she saw the importance of helping women and children in all the states learn more about missions. No matter what issues she dealt with while working with convention leaders, there were also constant demands on her time and skills from societies and churches all over the country. Thank goodness she rarely traveled alone. Sister Alice accompanied her on many trips, but for longer trips, she had a delightful travel companion, Anna Schimp. Anna's favorite trips were like Annie's — to the frontier and the reservations.

They somehow squeezed in three more long trips west in the following three years.

Along with all the traveling and speaking and writing, Annie recognized a looming crisis just under the surface. There had long been talk of a training school for women who felt called to mission service. The way to go about this training, however, was a matter of growing discussion among Baptist women everywhere. Annie had so much to do that she could not focus enough time on this pressing need. She also realized that a lot of women did not share her views on how and where to do such training. Annie grew more worried and stressed each year as she saw this issue in need of a solution.

Free time was something the Armstrong sisters had too little of. Their older sister, Mamie Armstrong Levering, loved to spend time with Annie and Alice. However, chances for the three sisters to be together were rare. Annie was often traveling in her job, and Alice was busy with her writing responsibilities. Together moments for the sisters were cherished because they were all too infrequent. However, one special Saturday night in May, Annie and Alice enjoyed a meal with Mamie and then visited in her lovely parlor. Mamie knew Annie so well that she could tell that something was clearly bothering her. "Annie," she spoke, "I can tell something is disturbing you. Please tell me." Mamie glanced at Alice, and she, too, was nodding and wanting Annie to share with them. Annie gave a long sigh.

"Mamie," she spoke, "there is a big burden on my heart. I will try to make the story short. It isn't sweet, though. This problem is a bitter taste in my mouth," she grimaced and shook her head. "Several years ago, I got a letter from Dr. E.Z. Simmons. He is a missionary to China who was in America on furlough. He had worked out a plan," Annie related, "for a training school for Southern Baptist women who felt called to mission service. Brother Simmons had already developed his *whole* plan." Annie sounded indignant, "He just wanted my seal of approval!"

Mamie, knowing her sister well, quickly responded, "Annie, I have an idea he didn't get that stamp of approval."

"No!" Annie retorted. "His idea was too sudden. Furthermore, the details were not acceptable to our executive committee." Annie warmed up to her topic. "In fact," she added, "I had already been investigating the possibility of such a school for quite a while."

Annie's brow was even more wrinkled now, as she recalled the pain of the whole process. "Mamie," she explained, "Dr. Simmons didn't even wait to see what I thought, or what our WMU organization felt. He was busy traveling to the different states and talking to many pastors and leaders." Annie drew an indignant breath, "And he had *already* recruited students! This so-called school was to be at Louisville at the seminary." Annie shook her head in disbelief, "I have long felt we needed such training, but *not* at a seminary with men students."

Mamie quickly nodded in understanding, "Sister, I know it has been your feeling all these years that you would not speak at a meeting where men were present or go to school with men."

Annie quickly spoke up, "I know this isn't the feeling of many other women. However, I am unable to change this conviction of mine. I simply cannot." Shaking her head, she repeated, "This is just who I am." Mamie anxiously inquired, "So what happened next?

Annie quickly explained, "I proceeded to learn more. I even visited several training schools of other denominations to see how they were doing missions training for women." Annie sounded close to tears, and her frustration was obvious in her voice. "Why didn't Dr. Simmons first approach our organization, which was *founded* to help women be part of missions service? *Now* we learn that such a school is already in operation at our seminary in Louisville. It has been open for two years!" she sounded indignant. Annie continued explaining the situation. Several state papers had written articles about a women's training school, but Annie had no warning this was happening. A number of these articles were quite critical of Annie Armstrong and hurt her deeply. Her eyes welled with unshed tears as she confessed, "It is a fearful thing to be misunderstood." Both sisters knew Annie's mind was set. They knew when their Annie reached a decision, not to even try to change her mind. WMU women were lining up in groups; some of them supported Miss Armstrong because she was their beloved leader. Others felt that the great majority of Baptist women *wanted* a training school to be part of the existing seminary. Annie could scarcely keep her composure. She drew in a long breath and declared, "Alice, Mamie, I feel I must resign at our next annual meeting." By this time, Alice herself was close to tears. "Annie," she spoke softly, "the Union is your heart. You have poured seventeen years of your life into WMU. The women will not want you to leave."

Annie took another deep breath before admitting, "Sisters, I must confess to feeling hurt. My pride is hurt. How can I truly lead an organization that is promoting a policy to which I am strongly opposed? I just can't."

Mamie gave Annie a comforting hug as Alice softly suggested, "Annie, please," if you must resign at our May meeting, at least give a year's notice. That will give women a chance to look for a successor. And they will still have your guidance and wisdom while they search."

Annie sighed and concluded, "Sister, you are probably right. You usually are. I fear that my remaining indefinitely as leader would only create an open division in WMU. I feel compelled to retire and not bring about division."

Annie had made up her mind, and Alice simply tried to be there for her dear sister, to support her in any way she could. May 1905 arrived. Annie wished she could just simply not attend the annual meeting.

She would much prefer to write her resignation letter and have it read. Instead, she scolded herself for being a coward, and she and Alice boarded a train for Kansas City.

There was much excitement and chatter as the annual meeting convened. Most of the women knew there would be important discussion about seminary training for women. There could possibly be an endorsement of the school in Louisville. Annie gritted her teeth and quietly tried to go about business as usual. She knew what she must do. It was one of the hardest choices she had ever faced in life. WMU *was* her life, and now these years were coming to an end for her. Annie realized that the majority of the state leaders were in favor of the seminary. However, she was also aware that others would support *her* viewpoint simply out of loyalty to her as their leader. That would not benefit her beloved WMU.

In the business session, the women voted to re-elect Annie Armstrong as executive secretary and Lilly Barker as president. Annie quietly rose to her full height, then paused to take a sustaining breath. There was not a sound in the room as Annie informed the delegates that she would serve one more year. At the end of that year, she would step down. Immediately, Mrs. Barker rose and made a similar statement. The silence was stunning. No one had expected this. Many of the women looked at each other in shock. Annie spoke into the silence, "There is to be no discussion. My decision is final." Annie then requested the women to not ask her questions. "Please do not write to ask me why I have made this decision. If you write, know that I will not answer."

Alice likewise resigned as editor of the important material she prepared for several journals. No one doubted that Alice Armstrong meant what she said as well. Too much was occurring too quickly. The delegates could scarcely take it in. At the conclusion of the meeting, Alice and Annie boarded the train for Baltimore. The two sisters, so attuned in heart and spirit, looked at each other, then sank back on the cushioned train seats. Alice reached over and grasped her sister's hand. For long minutes, not a word was said. It was as if they were already saying goodbye to that work which had been their lives.

Annie finally spoke, "Sister, I am making a promise. I vow that this year will be the best *ever* in Woman's Missionary Union." Alice's eyes welled with tears of sympathy, as she responded, "Annie, I have no doubt that it will be a stellar year. You have been a stellar leader."

Annie Armstrong set about at once to make sure that statement was true. Being even busier than the usual rush kept Annie from having too much time to reflect. Reflecting hurt. She felt there had been too much turmoil already. Her answer was added work. Many days, Alice would look with dismay at her sister's busy pace and increasing tasks. Alice would silently shake her head, praying Annie would have strength to keep going.

One afternoon, Annie, the prolific letter writer, wrote a long note to a dear friend in another state. She felt the need to unburden her heart. She wrote, "I would rather have love than anything else that this world can offer. I sometimes think that it takes the dark days to help us to appreciate the sunshine, and perhaps trouble may be allowed that we may recognize more fully our Heavenly Father's love. And also that there is such a thing as genuine human affection." Before concluding, Annie wrote, "I was thinking this morning how I wished I could be Rip Van Winkle until this time next year, when I would be free from all connection with SBC (Southern Baptist Convention) mission work. I dread inexpressibly the next six months. I expect, though, strength will be given to go through with whatever comes."

The realization of a long-held dream was one special answer to her prayers for guidance. She had hoped and tried for years to see a home provided for children of missionaries. There were a number of MKs (missionaries' kids) in need of an education and loving care while their parents were serving far away overseas. Fall 1905 arrived, and Annie participated in the beautiful dedication service of the Margaret Home. It was a lovely house set on six acres of lawn and garden in Greenville, South Carolina. Both the mother and the daughter of the donor were named Margaret. Annie had worked tirelessly on appointing committees to work on every little detail, from finding the perfect "mother" for the children, to furnishing the home, to getting scholarships set up for the children to attend Baptist universities. Annie's heart sang with gratitude to see this dream become reality.

However, Annie's final trip to her beloved frontier and Oklahoma Territory was her heart's most treasured adventure that final year. She wanted one more time to strengthen ties with sisters on the frontier who were faithfully supporting missions. They were particularly dear to her heart. Annie cherished the days she spent on several reservations. Part of her time was spent meeting with the Delaware Indian Association. It gave her spirits a true lift. So did her time with the Kiowa tribe, who were reaching out to share the gospel on other nearby reservations. Annie was deeply touched to see how the various tribes had grown in faith in just a short few years and were actively sharing the gospel. Boarding the train to head back east brought a lump to Annie's throat. She knew she would not be back another time. Her heart ached, even as she smiled and waved farewell to friends who had become part of her life.

Typical Annie, she was barely home in Baltimore until it was time to head to another long-hoped-for trip. She was going with Rev. A.E. Brown, who headed up mountain work for the Home Mission Board. It was a nineteen-day trip and a real eye-opener to Annie. Here was another long-cherished dream — a chance to work with the eager, good-hearted people in remote areas who wanted to be a real part of

God's work. She fell in love with the eager, bright-eyed children in the mountain schools. Nearly all of them lived in bare dormitories, because there were no schools available near their homes. This was their chance at an education. They didn't want to waste it. Annie wrote a leaflet describing the Baptist schools and the children, nearly 4,000 of them scattered throughout five Southern states. Annie also discovered that some of the mountain areas to which she traveled were nearly impossible to get to in March weather. This journey to Kentucky and Tennessee and nearby states was a kind of vision trip for Annie Armstrong. She was a keen observer and discovered all sorts of ways WMU women could help in such a ministry. Annie, as the psalmist stated, "lifted up her eyes unto the hills," and saw need and hope and ways to make a difference. Those nineteen days, even the terrible roads included, were part of an unforgettable chapter in her ministry.

Every week brought opportunities to speak and challenge women to be all that God wanted them to be. Annie spoke in many churches about her two favorite new projects. These new projects made her smile as she recalled those first two home and foreign missions projects with which she galvanized women that first year, nearly eighteen years earlier. The brick cards for a church in Cuba and the offering to send two new missionaries to China had been amazing successes.

Now she challenged women to give a special offering as a memorial to Dr. Tichenor, who had so wonderfully led the Home Mission Board for many years. The money would be for the Church Loan Fund, so dear to his heart. The other project was for an offering to build a men's ward at the brand-new Yangchow Hospital founded just four years earlier. That was where her cousin, Mary Grace Levering Evans, and her husband, Phillip, had planted their lives. Both offerings were a success. That was no surprise. Creative and enterprising leader Annie Armstrong had spent eighteen years successfully guiding Baptists to magnificent service. The giving ability and passion of Baptist women set the standard for giving in the entire Southern Baptist Convention.

In spite of her inner turmoil, there is no question that Annie Armstrong's final year was remarkable. She drove herself tirelessly to pour into women her passion and enthusiasm for serving and giving and going. Occasionally, in an odd free moment, she reflected on her years of service. Annie revealed some of her feelings in a letter to a friend.

"I think," she began, "I realize more than I ever did, how necessary it is in mission work to recognize the frailty of human instrumentality and the absolute *necessity* of relying wholly on our Heavenly Father for direction every step of the way." Annie ended her letter by confessing to this friend, "I do not know whether it is a case of physical exhaustion, but I have rarely felt more incapable of going forward. Jonah is not my ideal biblical character, but I might be tempted to follow his example, if I did not fear a similar fate." Annie did not realize that she had put her finger on the very cause of many of her problems: She was absolutely exhausted, both physically and mentally.

One evening in late April, the two sisters had a rare evening at home. Alice grinned as they moved to the living room after a simple meal, "Sister, I had forgotten what it felt like, just the two of us, a leisurely evening at home."

Annie sighed as she sank into the comfortable overstuffed chair that had been their mama's favorite, "Alice, I am anticipating how wonderful it will feel quite soon, to actually have more time like this. These past ten or so months have been so very full of work and travel." Then on a sigh she finished, "But, Sister, also far too much stress. I admit it. And, I confess, Alice, I do dread going to Chattanooga. It's our last meeting." Her eyes filled with unshed tears, and tender-hearted Alice felt her own tears well up. Annie's pain was her pain as well. The sisters, so keenly tuned to one another, knew this chapter of their lives was closing.

"Annie," Alice's voice was gentle, "just think how God has blessed this year. One of your amazing talents is the ability to raise funds. Remind me how much we have raised for missions this year."

Annie was happy to recall an especially satisfying report that had just reached her desk. "Sister," and a smile spread across her face as she spoke, "I received the treasurer's report this afternoon. Just this one year, our women have raised over $152,000. That is more than we have ever given." Then she added, "Another big number has marked this year as well. My miles traveled make me tired to remember — 20,000 of them!" Annie recognized her inner sorrow at stepping down from leadership. But there were so many bright spots in this final year; she could thank God. It had been a wonderful year.

Nonetheless, boarding that train for the May 1906 meeting, Annie's legs felt like lead. After eighteen years, this last gathering seemed so very final to her. If only she could skip this meeting. The thought raced across her mind, and she instantly tossed it out. She was no coward. God had gone before her. He had led all these years, and He would continue to do so. Annie rested her heart on that thought.

The morning of May 10 arrived, and Annie wore a new charcoal gray silk skirt and blouse. With her hair piled high in its usual braids, she looked crisp and fresh. None of her inner sadness showed on her calm face. Annie read to the delegates a brief summary of the eighteen years of their organization. She smiled as she recalled their first year as Woman's Missionary Union back in 1888. She traced the hand of God leading them step by step. Annie recalled their tremendous growth and how women had made a remarkable impact on Southern Baptist life. She smiled broadly as she recalled the giving and going and growth of those eighteen years. Each woman in that sanctuary was stirred, many to tears, to realize how much God had blessed their work. This morning, there was present a handful of women who had been at that very first gathering in 1888, and they smiled to recall what the Lord had done through them.

The second day of the meeting, Annie stood before her beloved Union for the last time. She could read the sadness on many dear faces. They echoed the pain of parting that Annie herself felt. Making a few brief remarks, Annie officially handed over the assets of WMU to the Union. She paused briefly, then led in a short prayer of gratitude for God's many blessings. Annie closed by asking for His guidance and watch-care. With a small smile that somehow prevailed over the tears threatening to fall, Annie retired from the sanctuary.

The two sisters did not converse as they boarded the train for Baltimore. Finally settled in their seats, both leaned back and each gave a long sigh. Alice reached over and gently laid her hand on Annie's knee. Annie grasped her sister's hand and held it tightly. No words were needed.

Hours later that May night, the two sisters wearily entered their home of many years. Alice spoke as Annie started up the stairs, "Sister, tonight is sad after giving eighteen years of your life to those women."

Annie turned on the stairs and smiled gently. "Alice, I didn't give these years to the women. I gave them to God. The work is in His keeping."

The Rest of the Story — 1918

Annie was quietly seated in the monthly meeting of her church's Woman's Missionary Society. These days, she did not lead but always attended as one of the faithful members. That morning, the discussion was about the yearly Christmas offering for foreign missions. Annie inwardly smiled as she recalled 1888 when women had made the first offering for foreign missionaries. Come to think of it, that had been exactly fifty years ago! Annie, still tall and regal fifty years after that first offering, rose to her feet to speak. The women were quite surprised. These days, their Miss Armstrong seldom made any comments during meetings. When Miss Annie spoke, everyone was at attention. In a quiet but firm voice, Annie said, "I move that we ask that the annual Christmas offering be named the Lottie Moon Christmas Offering. The offering was first made at Miss Moon's request." There was a buzz of whispers and a nodding of heads as the ladies enthusiastically responded, voting unanimously to make the recommendation. And that became the name of what has become the largest single offering for international missions in the world.

Cecil Apartments, Annie's last home – right next to Eutaw Place Church, her church for many years. (Courtesy of National Woman's Missionary Union)

Epilogue

In 1906, Annie Armstrong stepped down after eighteen years as executive secretary of Woman's Missionary Union. That summer, a state Baptist paper published an article praising her years of service. The editor could have had no idea that his was a prophetic voice. The article declared: "The name 'Annie Armstrong' will always be a household word among Southern Baptists, and her memory will be frequent through the long years to come. Through her life and the forces she put in motion, this pioneer woman's missions leader left a great legacy to Southern Baptists." Sure enough, over a century (and even a millennium) later, Annie Armstrong's name is possibly the most recognizable of any name in North American missions. Without a doubt, she was the one woman, more than any other, who shaped Southern Baptist life.

Annie herself would be astounded. She felt herself unappreciated and quite misunderstood among her fellow Baptists in 1906. She had just left the job she loved and the beloved desk where she had fun writing, working, and planning for Baptist missions. Annie knew, however, that God still had plans for her. Indeed, He did. She stepped right back into the many roles she had held in her church since the day she gave her heart to Christ.

Best of all, she had time to work with her beloved "Little Folks," the Sunday school children. To those children, from preschoolers to junior high youth, she was not the capable and brilliant leader of Baptist women. She was their Miss Annie — who expected obedience and attention, and who loved them without reserve. From her, they memorized countless verses of Scripture, which stayed with them for life. Miss Annie and Miss Alice provided the most wonderful tea parties at their home, complete with real tea from real silver pots, and served with dainty goodies.

Annie now had time once again to teach and love on the little orphan children at the Home for the Friendless, and to work with the many needy people at Bayview Mission. Annie had been tireless all her eighteen years of leadership among Baptist women across America. Now she was just as tireless back home, leading the weekly Mother's Meeting she had first organized when she was just a very young woman herself. She led those meetings for an astounding total of 42 years.

Annie was also manager for the Home for the Aged. It surprised no one who knew them that Annie and Alice made the usual team, working together and complementing each other's work in a multitude of ministries. Gentle Alice was always her sister's "good conscience," smoothing over the rough spots when Annie was impatient or hasty in temper.

Annie regularly attended her church's missionary society, but always as a member, quietly refraining from being a leader. Nonetheless, she remained keenly aware of what was going on in missions and what Baptist women were doing. She remained in the background, being careful not to attempt to direct others, but simply to support and pray for their work. Annie had laid an amazing foundation, far better than she could have imagined.

Time always brings inevitable change, and so it was for Annie Armstrong. Her hair was now streaked with silvery gray but still worn in her signature braids sitting high on her head. However, there was no change in the perfect posture she had learned from her mother a lifetime ago. Still tall, erect, and stately as she moved, Annie continued to wear floor-length dresses. (After all, that is how she had always dressed, even when riding on horseback on the range in Oklahoma!) And one last time, Annie and Alice returned to their beloved annual Cherry Meeting. Memories came flooding back to Annie as they walked the pathway to the entrance of Sater's Church, founded in 1742. She recalled the little 10-year-old girl who had raced from the carriage to the cherry trees long ago. The child Annie had heedlessly climbed the trees to pick sweet, plump cherries. Now the tall, elderly Annie, leaning only slightly on her elegant walking cane, simply reached up to pluck a cherry. They were still juicy and sweet, just as were the memories of the little girl who had dreamed so many dreams. And, yes, so many of those dreams had come to pass.

In 1915, when Annie was 75, her beloved oldest sister, Mamie, passed away. Mamie had always been attentive to her younger sisters; she even remembered them in her passing. Mamie left an annuity for both Annie and Alice, and they were able to live comfortably the remainder of their years. There was a remarkable bond between those two sisters. They had been together all their lives.

In 1928, Alice could not survive the bronchial infections that had long plagued her. Annie had never known life without Alice. With Alice gone, she did not wish to remain alone now in the home they had shared for a lifetime. Annie moved to the comfortable Cecil Apartments that stood right next to her beloved Eutaw Place Church. What better spot to live than right next to the church that had been her spiritual home for as long as she could remember. There had never been a pastor there who did not love and appreciate the Armstrong family, and her current pastor, Dr. Clyde Atkins, was no exception. He visited Annie regularly and relied on her prayers and unconditional support. Dr. Atkins commented, "Even as her body weakened, her faith increased." And the little children still loved to visit Miss Annie, especially when she could no longer go to church. She remained their dearest Miss Annie. And Miss Annie always had a special jar full of hard candies just waiting for their visits.

Annie's heart never left Woman's Missionary Union. When she received letters from WMU leaders and other Baptist women, she eagerly learned what was going on across the country. When there was a visitor from WMU leadership, Annie immediately asked about WMU news and work and how she could best pray for the Union and for the convention. Annie's heart must have rejoiced to see how her efforts to get the leaders of all the boards to work in close cooperation had paid off. They had learned from Annie Armstrong that in unity there was strength.

The year 1938 arrived, and 88-year-old Annie was now bedridden — her mind as sharp as ever, however, and her eyes alive and sparkling. Her cousin, Harriet Levering, was a widow now and lived in Cecil Apartments as well. She was a great friend and source of companionship for Annie. The spring of 1938, Harriet came for a visit. Harriet often dropped by, but that day a visitor arrived with her: It was Miss Juliette Mather, the new Young People's Secretary of WMU, with headquarters now in Birmingham. Juliette, tiny, always walking with a spring in her step and with a genuine smile on her face, was honored to meet the legendary Miss Armstrong. Juliette, a direct lineal descendant of the famous Cotton Mather of Colonial American fame, had the same far-reaching Mather mind and spirit.

Miss Mather came with a special purpose. National WMU was preparing to celebrate its 50th anniversary, the Jubilee year. The women of WMU wanted a personal message from their remarkable founding leader. There had been no official word from Miss Armstrong since she stepped down in 1906, some thirty-two years earlier. Annie graciously agreed with Juliette's eager request.

Annie sent a loving message for each age group. "For the Union, I hope it may grow every year stronger and better … Speak unto the children of Israel that they go forward. For the Y.W.A. (the Young Woman's Auxiliary), my wish is that they grow in grace and in the knowledge of our Lord and Savior Jesus Christ. For the Girls' Auxiliary (Girls in Action,) commit to memory, 'For God So Loved the World that He gave His only begotten Son that whosoever believeth in Him should not perish but have eternal life …' and 'the Lord is my Shepherd.'" Juliette asked about the Royal Ambassadors, and Annie replied, "To the RAs, be strong in the Lord and in the power of His might." Then Annie added, "My message for the Sunbeams (Mission Friends) is the Shepherd Psalm." Annie concluded with a statement about the special offerings for missions: "After study of God's Word comes study of the fields. Then people pray. Then they give."

Just months later, in WMU's jubilee year, Annie Armstrong went to her heavenly home, secure in the knowledge that Baptist women in America were still deeply involved in sharing Christ as they continued their legacy beyond its first half century. The imprint of her dedicated service remains stamped on every aspect of Southern Baptist life. Annie Armstrong's legacy glows especially brightly each year as Baptists across the nation, young and old alike, give to the offering named for the woman who gave her life in service to a nation and world in need of the gospel message.

In Eutaw Place Church, arrow pointing to pew where Annie and her family always sat. (Courtesy of National Woman's Missionary Union)

BIBLIOGRAPHY
BOOKS AND ARTICLES

Barstow, Sammie. "Annie Armstrong: Her Legacy Lives in Oklahoma," *Missions Mosaic*. WMU (Birmingham, AL). June 2009 (pp. 7-11).

Buhlmaier, Marie. *Along the Highway of Service*. Second Edition. Home Mission Board (Atlanta, GA). 1924.

Butler, Cathy. *The Story of Annie Armstrong*. WMU (Birmingham, AL). 2004.

Davis, Kate T. "I Remember Miss Armstrong." *Royal Service*. WMU (Birmingham, AL). March 1949 (pp. 6-7).

Durham, Jaqueline. *Miss Strong Arm: The Story of Annie Armstrong*. Broadman Press (Nashville, TN). 1966.

Evans, Elizabeth Marshall. *Annie Armstrong*. WMU (Birmingham, AL). 1963.

Sorrill, Bobbie. *Annie Armstrong, Dreamer in Action*. Broadman Press (Nashville, TN). 1984.

www.ingramcontent.com/pod-product-compliance
Lightning Source LLC
Chambersburg PA
CBHW040315170426
43196CB00020B/2928